THE TEACHINGS OF
THE ANGEL OF
NORTH AMERICA
BOOK I: HOW TO SAVE YOUR SOUL
AND YOUR SOCIETY

About the Author

Patricia Ann Meyer is a professional educator and trainer who has worked in public education for the past two dozen years. She spent her early career teaching severely disabled children. Although she found this to be satisfying, her administrative skills quickly became apparent and she followed her path through a succession of managerial positions.

Her first child was born in 1985 and she completed her doctoral degree at the College of William and Mary in 1986. In 1989 while living in Tidewater, Virginia, she accepted a position in the Richmond area although her family was not able to move immediately. Two years of commuting 210 miles each day were to follow. The hardship of this and the hours of loneliness were a severe test of her stamina and perseverance. As is often the case, however, the trial produced a better person and a stronger individual emerged.

Pat is a mother of two and now lives in central Virginia with Jerry, her husband of twenty years. She and her family attend St. Michael's Catholic Church. A locus of strange attractors and dynamic leadership, it is a rare place where one can find meaning in prayer.

THE TEACHINGS OF
THE ANGEL OF
NORTH AMERICA
BOOK I: HOW TO SAVE YOUR SOUL
AND YOUR SOCIETY

BY

DR. PATRICIA ANN MEYER

WITH A FOREWORD BY
STEPHEN HAWLEY MARTIN
AND AN AFTERWORD BY
THE ANGEL OF NORTH AMERICA

THE OAKLEA PRESS

Richmond, Virginia

FIRST EDITION
First Printing, 1996

ISBN 0-9646601-0-5

FOREWORD

It will not surprise hundreds of thousands, perhaps even millions of people in North America to read that the end of our society may be at hand. Nor will it surprise them to learn that the end may come as the result of a natural catastrophe.

With the possible exception of the flood of Noah's day, a disaster like this one has not occurred within human memory. Nevertheless, what will soon take place has happened many times. Quick-frozen woolly mammoths discovered in Siberia in the 1930s, food still in their mouths and undigested in their stomachs, are one bit of evidence. Fossils of palm fronds in Antarctica are another. The event, of course, is a shift in location of the earth's magnetic poles.

According to The Angel of North America, the shift will be accompanied by a huge electrical storm that will wipe out telecommunications, computer installations and electronic equipment. Commerce as we know it will halt because the electronic transfer of funds may be impossible. Government will no longer have the ability to communicate. Anarchy may ensue unless we are prepared.

This is only part of the bad news. Relocation of the magnetic poles will cause the polar ice caps to shift, which will cause them to melt. This will result in the displacement of populations now inhabiting coastal regions and low-lying areas such as Florida and much of the Midwest. People will not die in floods because the melting process will take several years, but given the current path we as a society are on, they may kill each other fighting over limited land and resources. In this way, the technological advancement of the past few thousand years would be destroyed and a new dark age would begin.

The Angel tells us we can take heart, however, that society would begin again. It would arise from small bands of survivors. Mankind once again would have the opportunity to grow and develop anew and to rediscover forgotten technology. If copies of this book survive and are handed down, if the principles contained in it are taught to subsequent generations, perhaps mankind may get it right this time. Perhaps a new civilization would achieve the potential that exists today to move into a golden and enlightened age.

Some believe that May 5, 2000, is the day the shift in the poles will occur. Astronomers have established that on this day the planets of the inner solar system, plus the moon, will arrive in a straight line with the sun. This has not happened in hundreds of thousands of years. As a result, the combined gravity of Mars, Venus, Mercury, the moon and the sun will tug on the earth.

Others believe that the end of the Mayan calendar, the winter equinox of the year 2012, will mark the day. Other dates and times have been postulated. According to the Angel of North America, however, no one knows or can know the exact time or date except God. Not even the angels in heaven.

The good news, and there is good news, is that even though the pole shift may be inevitable, the catastrophe of anarchy and the resulting enormous loss of life does not have to occur. We have it within our power to avoid what indeed could come to pass.

How do I know all this? Over the course of several meetings, Pat and Jerry Meyer have shared with me the visions and information they have received from angels. The angels have urged them to get this information out to all who will listen. The angels cited me as one who could help them do so.

If you have read my nonfiction book, *Beyond Skepticism,* you know that I was raised to be a skeptic. Yet enough has happened in my life for me to become convinced of the existence of a nonphysical realm that supports and informs physical reality. I've learned to trust my intuition, which indicated to me that what the Meyers were saying was true. Nevertheless, I asked for a sign from God that would tell me whether what they were saying was fact or fiction. It came less than twenty-four hours later.

My wife and I are regular churchgoers, but on that Sunday we did not go to the church we normally attend. We went to a Presbyterian church where the newborn child of friends was to be christened. The scripture lesson on which the sermon was based that day was Matthew 24:36-44. It was a message spoken by Jesus:

"No one knows about that day or hour, not even the angels in heaven, nor the Son, but only the Father. As it was in the days of Noah, so it will be at the coming of the Son of Man. For in the days before the flood, people were eating and drinking, marrying and giving in marriage, up to the day Noah entered the ark; and they knew nothing about what would happen until the flood came and took them all away. That is how it will be at the coming of the Son of Man. Two men will be in the field; one will be taken and the other left. Two women will be grinding with a hand mill; one will be taken and the other left.

"Therefore keep watch, because you do not know on what day your Lord will come. But understand this: If the owner of the house had known at what time of night the thief was coming, he would have kept watch and would not have let his house be broken into. So you also must be ready, because the Son of Man will come at an hour when you do not expect him."

The goal of this book you hold is to alert the owner of the house (you and me and all our neighbors) and in so doing change the direction of our society so that we are able to survive this natural catastrophe—perhaps even to have it be something that brings us together in a positive way so that we emerge from it better than we were.

Psychics through the ages, including Nostradamus, Edgar Cayce and a host of others in recent years, have had visions of the apocalypse and have placed the date around the turning of this millennium. During the past fifteen years many people have channeled entities from the spirit world or from other realities who speak of something similar. The earliest such book of which I am aware is *The Book of One, The RA Material.* Published about 1980, it was followed by three more in a series. More recently, a series that has been selling briskly in the New Age market is one by Kryon, a channeled entity. Kryon also speaks of an imminent shifting of the magnetic poles. These are only two examples. Any New Age book store will have many more dealing with the coming end times. Maps are even available that show what still will be above water after the caps melt.

Volcanoes, earthquakes, floods and forest fires are nature's way of cleansing the environment, of tearing down the old to make way for the new. So, too, is the coming pole shift. Some are optimistic that this change in the earth will usher in a "New Age" that will be better than the one we are leaving. This is indeed possible. But it will not happen unless we change the direction we are headed. Whether psychics see a positive or a negative outcome, however, all agree the time is near—anywhere from "any day" to seventeen years from this writing.

The Angel of North America says that the "punishment" that ensues from the pole shift and melt down will be God's way of correcting an imbalance that Pat Meyer will discuss on the pages that follow. This punishment is something that in effect we will bring upon ourselves in that our reaction to this earth change could wipe out a large percentage of the population. But the punishment part of the scenario does not have to happen. We are being warned and as a result can avert it by changing our path. We can be the homeowner who knew the thief was coming.

I first met Pat at a writer's conference at the University of Richmond. She seemed to be a nice person. During a break we chatted on one of my favorite topics, metaphysics. On impulse, I gave her copies of a couple of my books, feeling somehow that our paths were meant to touch. So I was not surprised when she called two months later.

She said that it had taken her weeks to get up the nerve. She was afraid I would think she was crazy. She said that she and her husband had been visited by angels, that she now had an angel as a constant companion, and that the angels had urged her to contact me. It was the angels who had led us to meet at the writer's conference. They wanted her to write a book. She then told me of her husband's vision and the angels' warning.

I asked if she had ever been in a New Age book store. The shelves are full of such prophecies. Chances were that whatever they were telling her already had made it into print.

She and her husband were life-long Roman Catholics. They were unfamiliar with New Age book stores but she was relieved to hear that what they were not alone in experiencing this phenomenon.

I asked what was the message of the book they wanted

her to write?

How to avoid the punishment.

Now this was a topic that might be worthy of a book, so I agreed to meet with Pat and Jerry. Intuitively, I felt they were telling the truth. After several meetings and the confirmation I received, I agreed to publish the book you now hold provided I be allowed to talk with the angels. I felt it was imperative that I be an eye witness.

I indeed spoke with an angel. We covered a good deal of ground during the three and a half hours we spent talking. You'll have an opportunity to learn what I learned as you read this book, but I do wish to recount one thing we discussed, and that is how Jesus figures in to all of this. Christians as well as non-Christians need to hear the message and many Christians believe that if a spirit is speaking through a living human being, that spirit must either be a demon or Satan himself.

I asked The Angel to tell me about Jesus. Who was he?

God's son, God incarnate.

Why did he come to earth?

He came to give new rules for living. His coming marked the gift of the Holy Spirit. Before that, the Jews had been given laws or rules to live by. The situation with these laws had gotten out of hand. The rulers of Jewish society had become evil. Controlling others was their objective. They had lost sight of what the laws were for. They were using them to exercise power over others. Jesus' message was that we are to praise and pray to God, keep the Commandments and treat others as we would want to be treated. In other words, to help each other and to do good works. This is still what we must do. Moreover, the situation that triggered Jesus' coming is similar to what exists in our society today. We have too many laws. These laws are used to control us; they take away free will.

The evening after hearing this something happened that seemed staged to drive home the point. My family and

I had decided to have dinner at the cafe attached to a large supermarket near our home. I ordered a hamburger cooked medium rare.

"Sorry," I was told. "According to the law, the best I can do is medium well."

"You're kidding," I said. "Is that because this is a supermarket?"

"No. Restaurants aren't supposed to cook them less than medium well done either, although some of them break the law and give them to people the way they want. We used to, but we've been cracked down on lately."

So in a misguided and absurd attempt to protect us from ourselves, our Big Brother government is now telling us how we must have our hamburgers cooked. (I can see some demagogue politician saying, "If this law saves one fifty year old man from a stomach ache . . . ")

The point that was driven home was that the Jews had laws to cover just about every behavior, just as we now do at the end of the twentieth century. The episode in the cafe was a vivid reminder of their dietary laws which Christ spoke out against in Matthew 7:15 when he said, "Nothing outside a man can make him 'unclean' by going into him. Rather it is what comes out of a man that makes him unclean," and that God abolished through his angels by giving the apostle Peter a vision recounted in Acts 10:9-16. Peter, hungry and praying, saw heaven open and something like a large sheet being let down to earth with animals on it that Jews such as Peter were forbidden to eat. A voice told Peter to kill and eat, but Peter said he wasn't about to. These were "unclean" animals. Then the voice said, "Do not call anything impure that God has made clean." (Acts 10:15.)

The Angel explained that with Jesus' coming God gave man the gift of the Holy Spirit. We do not need laws for every contingency. We have the Commandments and we have the Spirit, which is now present in each of us. It is our connecting link to the energy that is God. We must use free will to be guided by it.

To get to heaven we must have strong souls, souls which have been filled because we have made the right choices, because we have allowed ourselves to be led by the Spirit. Each time we exercise free will to do what is right, the spirit in us grows.

The Angel said that we are here in physical reality for the sole purpose of making a choice. On earth we have free will. That choice is between God and the absence of God, the void, or, in other words, evil or Satan. We make that choice daily through our actions. This doesn't mean a score card is kept. Nobody racks up points they can then use as credit against former or future sins. When you choose God through your actions your soul fills. When you choose evil through your actions it empties. A person can feel his soul filling because of the joy and happiness and sense of fulfillment it brings. He can feel the Spirit growing within him. He can feel his connection to God becoming stronger. On the other hand, choosing evil empties a person until eventually he has no conscience, no connection to God, and his soul is so empty, literally, he may reach the conclusion that life has no meaning. It is not uncommon for someone in this state to commit suicide.

People with full souls go to be with God (heaven) when they die. People with empty souls go the other direction. They enter the void and are cut off from God for eternity. People in the middle either await judgment, which will come at the end of the earth, or get another opportunity to come to earth to fill their souls.

When I all heard this, I recalled Jesus' words in John, 4:14: "But whoever drinks the water I give him will never thirst. Indeed, the water I give him will become in him a spring of water welling up to eternal life."

Some of my New Age friends will argue that good and

evil are human concepts that do not in fact exist. They will quote the line from Hamlet, "There is nothing either good or bad, but thinking makes it so." Anyone who follows this logic will arrive at a point where gassing the Jews was an okay thing to do. After all, if you were a Jew-hater, it was good. Hitler and his cohorts certainly believed it was. This is the sort of thinking that has our society on the path to destruction.

Most New Agers will agree, however, that a higher self or soul exists in each of us that is in touch and in tune with the universal consciousness. They may call it intuition, but whatever the label, they know they will not go wrong when they act on what it tells them.

If you aren't sure what is said in this book is true, please consult the Spirit within you. Get in touch with your connecting link, your conscience, your "still small voice." Call it intuition if you like, but get in touch. Ask if the message of The Angel of North America is valid. Ask for a sign that will confirm or deny it. But ask. If you are sincere, you'll get an answer.

Time still exists for most of us to save our souls. Time also exists for society to change its ways and in so doing to avoid having to start over. But society is asleep at the wheel. If enough of us take this message seriously and act accordingly, we can turn the ocean liner of our collective destiny before it crashes against the rocks.

May this book be a tap on the shoulder. May it be the wake up call.

Stephen Hawley Martin
February, 1996

ACKNOWLEDGEMENTS

Although the message we deliver has been inspired, the effort required to do so has been plain hard work. Our editor, Stephen Hawley Martin, has given selflessly of his many talents in helping us to produce this document. He has been thoughtful and kind, and become our trusted friend over the past few months. We are grateful for his willingness to take on this project and for his commitment to helping us get the message out. We hope his efforts will be rewarded as he so justly deserves.

At the beginning, when my husband questioned his faith, it was so hard to talk to anyone, the strain was terrible. Juanita, we want to thank you from the bottom of our hearts for listening and sharing your unique wisdom with us. You've been more important to us than you realize. Thank you.

Contents

HOW THIS BOOK CAME TO BE

My husband started to hear the voices in December of 1991. One said, "Lie down. I have a message for you." This continued to occur. Yet he kept it a secret from me for nearly two years. Our marriage became strained as a result. Eventually, he sought help, but no one could.

At last, he told me what was happening. After speaking with friends, we read the book, *The Celestine Prophecy*. The message it contained calmed his fears. So one day he did lie down and he said, "Yes, I'll listen."

Then it began. The angels came to give us their message.

In the beginning the message the angels brought was solely for my husband. He told me that three angels appeared to him and said that they were messengers of God. He asked them questions, "Who are you? Is this real? Why did you choose me?"

They showed him a punishment. They told him that our society has become too wicked and has turned away from God. In order to reset the balance on the earth, God would send a punishment that would cleanse the wickedness from the land. He was shown that among the earthquakes and storms, among the flood and the drought, a storm would come and take away our ability to communicate. The earth would go through a drastic change and the water of the oceans would rise. The people would not be killed in the flood, but rather, they would kill each other because of the breakdown of our society. This made my husband believe.

The angels said they had chosen him to be a survivor. He was one of the just people who would be able to show others how to hold on to what we might have left. The angels remained with him for approximately four months preparing him; teaching him what he would need to know. Then their visitations ended. They seemed to be finished. The angel, whom he had come to know as The Teacher, said that he was now ready. He needed only to wait.

As he shared this experience with me I could not comprehend the thought of waiting. I asked to be a part of it. I asked what I could do to help prevent this punishment that would come to us. The Teacher warned me that once I had the message, my life would be changed irrevocably. She gave me time for reflection. After this, I agreed to carry the message to others.

The Teacher has been with me ever since. What I write here is only a portion of the message and the information I have received. It has been very difficult to choose what to say because there is so much. But in the hundreds of hours in the last two years that I have been in touch with The Teacher, or the Angel of North America as I will also refer to her, the core message has come in nearly every single discussion. Our society no longer accepts the existence of evil. We have let it become a part of us. Our liberal ideas have led us away from using our moral judgment. We have lost the meaning of life. God does not interfere with man. He has given us free will.

I asked her, "Why, then, have you come to us?"

Her reply was, "God will not send a punishment without giving his people warning, without giving them every opportunity to choose what is good. I am here to give that warning."

I asked if this is why there is so much emphasis on angels today. She said, no. She said that people have a sense that things are not right and they are looking for answers. They do not know where to turn. They are looking for spirituality everywhere. She told me that the goodness of God is within each of us and that we must pray and follow the Commandments and do good works for others in order to allow God's energy to come to us and fill our souls. This is how each of us personally can be saved.

What I have chosen to share with you in this book are some of the concerns that The Teacher would like for us as a society to focus upon. It is not enough to tell us that we have gone wrong and need to change. In an effort to be helpful, she has given us instructions concerning which aspects of our society are good, which need to be changed, and which are those that literally are destroying us because they are tearing us apart.

I have asked for signs to be given to me to confirm that what she was telling me was true. I wanted to be certain that I was not being deceived, that I could be confident that I was conveying God's message. During the past two years, she has told me weeks in advance of every change that would occur in my life. I can assure you that everything The Teacher has predicted has come to pass. As a result I cannot help but believe.

Both my husband and I were raised as Roman Catholics. We continue to be practicing Roman Catholics and attend St. Michael's Church. Some of you reading this may believe you see some Catholic bias in my writing. I assure you, however, the message The Teacher has for us is for all the people of our society regardless of race or religion, regardless of their beliefs. She wishes to speak to all people. The Teacher has not asked anyone to give up or change their faith. She assures us that God is not concerned with what particular church you go to as long as you believe in him.

One of the reasons for this teaching is to disparage many of the liberal concepts held by our society. The Teacher has assured me that God is not a "liberal." The "liberal attitude" as she defines it is one by which we accept anything that anyone else wants to do. It is an attitude that postulates that freedom should be without bounds. This liberal attitude gives rights without restrictions. It is one that discourages judgment of others' actions. This attitude has become so pervasive that it is the reason evil is growing in our society. We have abandoned our moral codes to it.

The Teacher tells us she has been bringing this same message to people throughout the ages. Unfortunately, I cannot possibly tell all in this first book that needs to be said. But it is important that I begin to deliver at least the core. I plan to bring more to you later. Part of my instruction is to continue helping people for the rest of my life or until the punishment comes. She has asked me to speak from the heart, in plain language that can be easily understood today.

Many of you may recognize aspects of our discussions from Bible passages. The Teacher has made no direct references to the Bible. I am not writing to compete with the Bible. The message that the teacher is giving me is for our society specifically at this time and for this time. It will have little meaning to the next generation if we make the necessary changes.

When she discussed these things The Teacher did not pull any punches. Her language was severe and forthright. There was a sense of urgency to her words in that certain prophecies will come to pass within my lifetime if changes are not made. God and the angels do not recognize time as we do, so it is not easy for me to comprehend precisely what The Teacher means by "urgent." I have been told, however, that this punishment, if it comes, will not be the end of the earth. Nevertheless, it may set in motion other events to make such prophecies come true. The Teacher is very careful about telling me the future. I have no idea what is in store for the earth. I only know the specific warnings she has given. It is quite clear that if we allow evil to continue to grow in our society, the imbalance will become too great and God will intervene to stop it. This, along with giving us the message of the meaning of life, is The Teacher's reason for coming to us.

I agreed to write this book and to accept the changes in my life because what she has shown me is so compelling that not to do so would have been virtually impossible. God's energy has flowed into me and given me the strength to make necessary changes in my life. I believed I had a good life before, but it has become so much better since I listened to the message. It is my sincere hope that in the short time we spend together that I can convey to you some of the same energy and power I have gained from this message.

As previously mentioned, this is only a portion of what the angel had to tell me. Per her instructions we will be building a retreat with the proceeds of this book to help people with the problems in their lives. If you have special needs, would like to be a part of this effort, or would like to be included in our prayers, you can write to me in care of The Oaklea Press, P. O. Box 29334, Richmond, Virginia 23242-0334. I look forward to hearing from you.

Now, let's begin.

21

THE NATURAL ORDER

As you might well imagine, when The Angel of North America first came with two others in an attempt to communicate with my husband, Jerry, he wondered whether or not he was going mad. Jerry is not an overly religious person in the usual sense of being an adamant churchgoer or dogmatic in his beliefs but he is what you might call spiritual. In his adult lifetime he has developed this aspect of himself through daily prayer and meditation. When he did agree to listen, the angels appeared as human forms before a white lit background, faces radiant and features indistinguishable.

Things I will write about here are controversial for our times. It may help you to know that I was quite liberal in my thinking both politically and in my views toward social issues prior to my lessons with The Teacher. As a result I had difficulty accepting much of what I was being told. Nevertheless, I have become a believer. You must judge for yourself what is right. That is your prerogative as one who has free will. I will say, however, that all of what is written here is true whether or not you believe or accept it. Not everyone will be saved nor will they change their ways as a result of these words. It is not necessary, nor is it the intent of this book. Just enough people need to change in order to right the balance of good and evil in our society today.

The only reference to the Bible I will make is to the Ten Commandments. These are as accurate and valid now as they were when Moses received them directly from God. They are the only laws we need. All other proper behavior should come as a result of our "listening" to what the spirit of God within us is saying at any given time or in any situation.

Before I begin relating to you the teachings of The Angel of North America, let me mention that as a matter of syntax I generally will refer to God as "he" and to our angels as "she" even though in spirit there is no sex. The Teacher, or The Angel of North America as I will refer to her in this book, explained that many, many angels exist. They are God's messengers and helpers. Each is given a specific task within God's angelic hierarchy. Some are responsible for helping specific individuals. Others are assigned to whole societies and become experts in these. The Angel of North America is the overseeing angel for the entire continent. She has held the position of teacher of God's law and purposes since the time of the first human beings on earth.

The purpose of life in the physical realm is for beings such as ourselves to have an environment in which we can exercise free will. Free will has no meaning in the spirit realm. Those in spirit, such as The Angel of North America, do God's will as a matter of course. They have already made their choice.

If you have not done so before, I suggest you begin thinking of yourself as a spirit who at present is having an experience in a realm away from your natural home. This realm apart is what we know as physical reality. This may seem odd at first because you probably have no memory of your existence prior to this life. This is as it should be because it is part of God's plan. When we are born on

THE TEN COMMANDMENTS

1. You shall have no other gods before me.
   (Put God first in your life.)

2. Do not worship idols.
   (Money can be an idol.)

3. Do not misuse the name of the Lord.

4. Remember the Sabbath and keep it holy.
   (You need to spend time resting and
   praying.)

5. Honor your mother and father.

6. Do not murder.

7. Do not commit adultry.

8. Do not steal.

9. Do not lie.

10. Do not covet what others have.

earth we come with amnesia.

In this realm of earth you no doubt perceive yourself to be separate and apart from God. You perceive that you have free will. It is indeed true that you can choose to do whatever you wish. God made it this way so that you would have the opportunity to choose him or not to choose him. This is why you are here. If you choose him, you will go to heaven. You will be with God. Eventually, you will be part of his New Creation. If you do not choose God, you will continue to exist, but you will exist apart for all eternity.

Many in our society today feel tired, depressed and unfulfilled. Yet they are good people who have not been taken over by evil. They want to know what is wrong. Many of these people know Jesus, they accept God in their lives, but they have a feeling that their life just isn't right, that there is more. There should be happiness. It is my hope and the hope of The Angel of North America that you will find the answers you are seeking in this book and in others that will follow.

God has a natural order for everything that happens on the earth. When people are synchronized with this natural order peace and harmony are to be expected because that is the way life is supposed to be. When this natural order is interrupted or changed, the harmony is no longer there. Tension and conflict exist because the natural order wants to reassert itself. This is the situation today in our society. The natural order is God's law and takes precedence over anything man does.

With regard to this feeling of unhappiness, many say that they want to get back to a simpler time. They are willing to give up aspects of their lives to be able to regain control. Unfortunately, more than simply giving up the pursuit of material goods will be necessary to make them happy.

During a person's life there are certain tasks that need

25

to be completed. Growing up and maturing into an adult is one. Today, there is no longer a time, a ceremony, a point of departure for most when people are expected to make the change from childhood to adulthood.

Life cycles are part of the natural order. This means that tasks must be completed. Ideas develop, evolve and outlive their usefulness. Change then will occur and the idea will either die, or a new one will evolve if a need for it still exists.

The natural order is for people to find a mate, to have children, to grow old together and to stay together until one of the couple dies. This is the natural order. It is the natural order for there to be a completion date, for people to understand what to expect and to plan accordingly. Unhappiness stems not just from seeking only material goods that have no lasting value, but from having a life that has no stages by which to measure progress. The society is ruining itself by adopting the attitude that people and the events in their lives are commodities to be traded, that they have a monetary value which can be placed on them.

Another important part of the natural order is work. People used to develop and train themselves to perform a task that was useful to society. No longer is there an expectation of this. Today, we talk about ongoing training so that an individual is always ready for the next type of work that is developing. For many, work no longer means anything. Corporations, these soulless phantom entities, use people's lives as a commodity to make profit. Instead of people working and having pride in their work and an understanding that what they do accomplishes something, their work has been devalued to a portion of bottom line profit. When it becomes too easy to replace an employee, that person's life has no meaning with respect to the work they do. Since the time of the metaphorical story of Adam and Eve, when they were sent out of the garden, work has not only been necessary but it has been and was meant to be be a fulfilling part of life.

When companies have power over people, for that portion of time that they control people's lives they need to respect and foster a cycle of work for each employee. Instead, the concept of keeping up with the competition, of out pacing the competition, of beating the competition has become the rule. Each corporation is chasing that elusive dream but can never quite reach it. Change does not come because change is necessary or change is good. Change comes about for the sake of change. There are no more long term plans or goals. Life cycles have been reduced to months. The life cycle of a product or service is now so short people cannot conceive of planning their life around their work. This causes tension. It is a source of unhappiness.

Most people believe that when they have given up their fast-track life they will feel better because they have more control over their lives. If a person can get control back after they have given it away, they will have made a positive and right move toward regaining their soul. Having their soul back and being able to use free will to make choices will make them feel good, but it is not all that is necessary for happiness to come. People are weary because so many in the society have to fight against the corruption of the natural order.

People need and want to have things finished in their lives. People need and want to be able to plan. According to The Teacher the government experiment of social security that was started two generations ago was the single most powerful event in the changing of society for the worse. In an effort to help people, the government took away the need for people to plan their lives. It took responsibility from employers for the care of people when they no longer were able to work or retired. Now there was something else to take care of workers when they were no longer needed. This broke down the sense of family between workers and employers. The bond between employer and employee became less and less important. Eventually, the labor of individuals became a commodity. This is what people cannot run from today. There is no place people can go to feel that their work is their life. There are exceptions of course. The point is that for the bulk of society the bond of trust and mutual respect between worker and employer no longer exists. And yet it is the first bond that people need to form upon becoming adults. This bond is a most important aspect of adult life because people need to work. All the other aspects of life come from and are satisfied by work. If this part of the natural order cannot be satisfied, people will never be happy.

Change needs to come more slowly. Society needs to readjust its thinking, not to stop progress, not to stop making life better for everyone, but to stop making changes for the sake of change. Once again people need to experience a sense of completion with the tasks that they do. They need this throughout their lives at each point of natural transition. This is the natural order.

Following established customs and traditions can help offset the negative effects of change. These are long-term ideas and rituals that bind a society together through generations, through centuries, through a millennium. Customs and traditions do not change, they evolve. A custom that existed two hundred years ago may no longer be valid today. Nevertheless, if people still adhere to it, it is glue that binds the people of the society together. It gives meaning to their lives and a sense of completion each time they participate in the custom. It is a necessary part of life. It is part of the natural order that God gave to Abraham, the first of his chosen people.

No matter who you are or where you live, no matter what your custom may be, it binds you to God. It is part of the natural order. It is evidence that you accept God's way and that God accepts you in his love.

When the society goes against tradition, when it ignores tradition, or tradition is trivialized, the sense of completion is taken from people's lives. This goes against the natural order. There is a sense of loss. People will be unhappy until the natural order is restored.

People in a society need to have similar traditions. They need to participate in the traditions in order to keep their society alive and growing. One of the problems today with respect to race relations is that there are not common customs and traditions that bind all our people together. People cannot be a society when they are separated and want to cling to disparate customs.

As people migrate around the world they often maintain the customs of their homeland. These people will remain unhappy. When they keep old customs they will not become a part of a new society into which they move. To become integrated they must adopt the customs of the new society. Otherwise, they will not fit in; will not be accepted. If they have shown that they cling only to their old customs, they will not be invited to participate in the local customs, and there can no longer be completion to certain aspects of their lives. People in this situation will always have a longing for their homeland. This is the natural order.

The natural order is to come to and to recognize completion of the different aspects of one's life. Because things are changing so fast in our society, often people forget about and leave behind old customs. This leaves loose ends dangling and results in discontent and unhappiness. Often in our modern society, people are left without meaningful work. When they do not have the fulfillment of work and find themselves in broken families and with broken vows, there can be no doubt that the result will be unhappiness and longing.

Another aspect of the natural order is marriage. Marriage has become disposable or even unnecessary. This is an attitude that is wrong and destructive. Almost every religion and marriage ceremony states that marriage is a scared and a solemn vow. Marriage is referred to in the Commandments. It is a departure step in a person's life that should end only in death. It should not end because of unhappiness, because of unwillingness to compromise, because of losing a job or even because of adultery. Divorce goes against the natural order. It is the natural order that when people make the commitment to marry, they stay together for life. According to The Angel of North America there is no room for argument on this. There can be no accepting of excuses. The Teacher realizes that things happen, that marriages do not always work, that people make mistakes. God knows this, too. But when it happens, it goes against the natural order.

As has been said, people often are unhappy in their lives because certain aspects of the natural order are not satisfied. When people divorce, this is the case. If you are divorced and remarried, if you are living together outside of marriage or in any of today's liberal alternative families, you are living your life against the natural order. You are swimming upstream and your life will be more difficult than is necessary. You are in a situation wherein no matter what you do, you cannot bring to completion the vow you made at your marriage ceremony.

What sets man apart from the animals is his soul. With a soul comes free will and free will carries with it a responsibility to make choices. No matter what anyone says, the actions you take in life are your choice.

The people in this society make choices by electing their leaders. When they make bad choices it is the society's responsibility to undo what those bad leaders may have done to the society. Overall it is everyone's responsibility to do what is right and good for everyone else. This is rule number two of the new rules which have been given by the Angel of North America as a messenger from God. The new rules are:

1. Obey the commandments.
2. Do good works to help other people.
3. Pray to God.

The objective is for us to simplify our lives. As a devotee to and a messenger of God, The Angel of North America is not making a judgment against people who are divorced. She has come to tell us that problems in our lives arise from having unfinished aspects left dangling. Divorce is a problem of the society that needs to be changed. It will not be changed tomorrow. Nor can anyone undo damage that already has been done. But the situation does not have to get worse.

She has come to give us the information we need to help us in making the right choices in our lives and to help us save our society from having to be punished because too much evil has grown within it.

It is true that staying married to the same person all your life will not assure happiness. If a poor choice was made in a mate, of course there will be unhappiness. This means that you must be very careful when you choose. Do not do things that tempt the natural order. Do not marry a person whose beliefs conflict with yours or with those of your family or with the goals you have set for your life. Instead, keep in mind the vow, "Until death do us part." Marry with the idea of completion in mind. Everyone in love feels that their love will last forever. But there is more to a successful marriage than love. What is important is your mate's soul.

The need for completion is very real and very important. Yet people have created in the government a way to relieve themselves of the responsibility of their vows and thereby to thwart this. Your vow may be absolved on paper. It can be done so through the courts. It may be sanctioned by the government. But divorce is against the natural order because what you began will not be carried through to its natural end. It is a major reason people in our society feel sad and unfulfilled.

GOD'S PLAN

God does not want people to fail. But he does not want to make things too easy for us either. We are here as a test. For mankind to advance to a higher order there must be a struggle. Science and technology are part of this. Technology can be very good and beneficial in our struggle, but we must be careful that a balance is maintained between technology and God's natural order. Otherwise God may intervene to reset the balance. When we use technology to overcome the natural order, for example, we invite evil in. We are tempting God to destroy what we have built. A punishment will come to teach us that we are on the wrong path and that we need to reset our sights and to reevaluate our goals.

Punishments have come before. A punishment always is so severe that it enables survivors to overcome the evil that society has allowed into it. This allows them to start with a clean slate. Those who remain again will have a fair opportunity to make choices and to choose properly. The proper choices always lead to God. This, for example, was the basis of the renaissance.

In order to put the present into perspective, The Teacher has given us some perspective on the history of man from her point of view. For many years people were pagans. Then God came and gave them a new message. Unfortunately there was not a society or a culture which accepted the message that was strong enough to maintain and advance it. The Romans had a great culture that was capable. If they had given up their pagan ways and had accepted the teachings of Jesus, The Teacher tells us it would be very likely we would all be speaking Latin today. But there was no strong leader. There was no powerful culture that accepted the new rules.

Nearly a thousand years passed and mankind essentially treaded water. It took the threat of a similar religious belief in the form of Islam to congeal the society. The people of the western world felt they had to fight this other religious belief. The society of Europe grew out of the struggle that ensued. When the struggle ended and people felt they had conquered evil, two new great societies arose. Both the European and the Moslem worlds underwent a renaissance. This renaissance in the east and in the west took place because both societies were strong in their respective faiths. Both adhered to the message that God had given them. Their societies progressed beyond the wildest imagination of anyone. Churches and Mosques rivaled each other. Technology grew to the point that it could no longer be contained. The artistic endeavors, the advancements in mathematics and science that took place form the basis of our culture today. People still marvel at the advancements that were made.

The Teacher tells us that we are on the brink of another conflict between east and west. If we pursue the impending conflict between the Moslem and the Christian worlds there will be great destruction and disorder. A new renaissance will grow out of this conflict but it will take hundreds of years to be realized. A better alternative is for all societies of the world to work together. Rather than for destruction, we can use our technology to enhance the natural order. Within a generation we can take a giant step ahead in the evolution of mankind.

God does not like to interfere in our world. The Renaissance was not God's doing. It was a blossoming of the human spirit. God's role was to send a punishment and afterward to let the people decide their own direction. Because people began to spend their lives glorifying God, God gave them the knowledge and the inspiration to do great things.

The people of those times had a deep sense of spirituality. They had a concept of God and of the realm of heaven. Spirituality was ingrained in daily life, a deep and important part of it. Businesses flourished as a result. Communities grew. Unbelievable riches accrued. Ancient arts were rediscovered. Some of the most beautiful and long lasting art was created during this period.

Consider for a moment the works of art from that epoch and what so called artists produce today. During the renaissance artists painted pictures of God or angels, of Jesus and Mary. They made statues glorifying God and his image. Artists were striving to give their patrons glimpses of the spiritual or mystical. This is a noble and authentic goal.

Today people literally put together piles of trash and call it art. They spray paint on a canvas with a ketchup bottle and call it art. They glorify homosexuality and call it art. There can be little doubt that our society today is in the toilet. This is because belief in the spiritual aspect of reality is everything and our society by and large rejects it. It is why when people were truly afraid of evil during the renaissance, some of the world's greatest advances were made.

Many today think evil is superstition. They believe that only a fool would be concerned about it. The Teacher has asked us to consider what great works of art are being created in our society. She has asked, "How will future generations view your society? What ideas or accomplishments will endure for future generations to build upon? What wondrous buildings are being designed and constructed that can compare in terms of durability and beauty to the cathedrals of the Renaissance?"

Even so, mankind is on the verge of the next step in his evolution. People are excited and afraid at the same time because they can feel within them that we are on the brink of a new era. We can take this step but it will require dramatic changes in our society. We must change in order to make it happen or God will bring a punishment so that in the future people will have the opportunity to take the step.

We are told by The Teacher that the next step is beyond what almost anyone has imagined. It is not the discovery of inner peace. It is not the solving of the problem of poverty in our own backyard. It is a step that is expensive and dangerous. It is a step that will take us past what we now know to a new level of understanding. At last we will understand where mankind is to go.

We are told by The Teacher that by looking back we can get a glimpse of what lies ahead. Man's quest has always been to go where he has not been before. For Eastern cultures this was to discover Africa. For Europeans it was to discover America. Of course, human beings already lived in both these places, but the perception was that these lands were unknown. They represented the "great beyond." There was incredible risk involved in their exploration. There was great expense and the certainty of loss of life. There were many reasons for this adventure. Knowledge, science, trade, and conquering new lands for the king and for God.

People now have conquered the world. There is no place left that is unexplored. There are few mysteries to be solved. But the spirit of adventure still lives. This spark should not be extinguished by business or by government. People want to do more and there is more to do.

Our quest must take us beyond the earth. Imagine what it will be like to be travelers in space. We are told by The Angel of North America that this is the frontier toward which we must direct our efforts.

Imagine the problems to be solved which will present themselves. Imagine the challenge. It will be of the magnitude of the challenges that were faced by civilizations centuries ago when they set out to explore an uncharted world.

There is a force of energy that is difficult for us as humans to understand. Yet this force will be the key that will enable us to achieve our goal. The Teacher says this force is what we might think of as souls looking down on earth. It is an energy that flows throughout the universe. We are part of and connected to it.

This energy does not flow like water at a given speed. Rather, it is more a beingness that is present everywhere at once just as electricity is everywhere at once within an electric grid. Learning to understand this energy and how to use it will make space travel both possible and practical.

There are other places to go, other places to see. There are other worlds to conquer. The Teacher tells us that she and the other angels wonder what is holding humans on the earth. They wonder, "Why are they waiting? What is holding them back? Why don't they try to leave their world to explore others?"

If there are others in the universe, they may be waiting for us to take the first steps away from our planet. There may be meeting places just beyond where we will see new worlds. New possibilities will open to us.

Five hundred years ago, a good portion of the population, including the leaders of the Church, believed that the world was flat. They believed that if a ship sailed too far out, it would fall off the edge of the earth.

The Teacher asks, "What is keeping you attached to the earth today? Why are you so afraid to move beyond your planet?"

Ever since man stepped on the moon, there has been a mood of entrenchment, a mood of fear. Saving the planet has become the number one concern of many. People believe that there is no where else to go. They are afraid that the universe is a hostile place. In 1491, many thought the same of the Atlantic Ocean. In 1900, people were thinking about flying but were not sure it could be done. In 1960, flying to the moon was science fiction.

We have stopped thinking beyond present boundaries. This is a cause of unhappiness and discontent. People yearn for a return to a time of adventure and exploration. There are a lot of reasons and a lot of people to blame for the state of the world and humanity. But The Teacher tells us that from the outside looking down on the earth it appears that there is no more than fear and the lack of will holding us back. She tells us this fear is produced by evil. Evil gets its strength from people giving away their free will to it. Primarily, free will is given to the government because people expect the government to care for them and to fulfill their needs.

The government is a soulless entity. The force of evil uses the power that the people have given to the government to keep them weak and drained. Evil does not want people to venture outside their realm. It does not want people to progress and to go beyond where they now are. It does not want man to gain knowledge beyond what he now knows. The very last thing evil wants is for people to go out from earth and discover the power of God. This is what is keeping us here on earth. It is not that the task is too big or too expensive. It is not that there are no people willing to sacrifice their lives for the advancement of mankind. No lack exists of people willing to try to do more. What is lacking is our conviction as a people. This, and our inability to find a leader who has the courage and the wisdom to lead us to places we have not been before.

These things are holding us back.

People have a long, long way to grow and to stretch out and they cannot do it any longer here on earth. People must overcome their fears. We are fearful of our livelihoods. We wonder, "Will we lose our jobs? Will our business fail?" We are afraid of getting sick. We are afraid of crime and of meanness in the world. We are afraid of poverty, of war, of hunger and disease.

In our society, people are afraid of lawyers. They are afraid of dying of cancer. People are afraid of being out of touch. They are afraid of being alone. They are afraid of being taken over. All these fears are a part of everyday life. They have become so overwhelming that people do not do anything but try to protect themselves. We have allowed ourselves to be put on the defensive. We have dug in.

The idea of taking a risk and suffering the consequences keeps people from doing what they want to do. People would like to feel more spiritual. They want to feel close to God. They want to feel a connection. People want to have friendships again. They want to enjoy a sense of community. But all of these things seem out of reach. They are indeed out of reach because we have given over our free will.

The attitude exists that there is always some expert who will take care of things for us, that a few phone calls or a visit to a government agency will somehow solve all our worldly problems. This is the giving over of our free will. When we give over free will to someone else or to some government agency, we are not making choices. We do not have the opportunity to receive the energy that God has available for us. We have cut ourselves off.

Lawyers thrive on this attitude of ours. Lawyers feel that because they follow the law, the law can solve everyone's problems. But laws do not solve the problems. Imagine you are a pioneer crossing the desert and the plains. You and those of your immediate group must solve your own problems. This is the attitude we must regain.

Lawyers use money to solve problems. Money is an inert, unfeeling tool that is used to control people's lives. This works in two ways. People who have money can be controlled because of their fear of losing it. People who do not have money can be controlled by money being withheld from them. People need to realize this to overcome their fears and retake control of their lives. They must stop allowing money to control them. This is not a difficult concept to comprehend. It does not mean that one has to live in poverty. It does mean that we have to start seeing bigger issues.

Consider, for example, product liability problems. It is generally believed in our society that if one is hurt by a product, the company that makes that product should be punished. The punishment will be to give the injured person a large sum of money. Yet corporations have no soul. They have no feelings. Punishment is not an effective deterrent to a corporation. If someone makes a product and intentionally tries to hurt you with it, the punishment of that person will do some good. But people generally do not try or intend to hurt one another.

This whole idea of punishing corporations perpetuates evil. It keeps people going around in circles and using up their lives. It keeps people from praying and seeing goodness. It perpetuates anger and animosity on the part of some toward soulless non-living entities that do not have feelings and do not care about anything except perhaps to drain the life force from people. Any lawyer reading this should stop and think what he is doing with his life if this sort of work is his livelihood. Lawyers help facilitate the process.

In a similar vein, one also can turn over free will to financial experts. These are people who claim they can help you make more money which will make your life secure. The fact is, they cannot guarantee anything. They certainly cannot guarantee to make your wealthy. They cannot guarantee security in your old age. They cannot guarantee you will not lose everything. Yet people by the millions trust their savings to financial analysts and so called experts in the hope of gaining more money. This puts others in control of an aspect of a person's life, and in this society the financial aspect is very important.

This is not to say that every financial analyst is a bad person. But allowing someone to have control over you and your life tempts corruption. The more people who give over portions of their lives to a particular analyst, the smaller the fraction of caring he will have to give to each of his customers. Regardless of what the commercials say or what the advertisements read, financial analysts are not God. They do not have the power and ability to be infinitely caring and fair in all dealings. Somewhere in the conscience of everyone is the thought, however small, that if they give money to someone, that person may not always use it in their best interest. People should listen to their consciences.

The Teacher tells us that when we give over responsibility for our money, a part of our energy is taken. Some of the ability is taken which enables us to connect fully with God. A bit of emptiness is left. We feel this but we cannot say exactly what it is. It is not so much that we mistrust. Nevertheless, something is holding us back from becoming the person we want to be. The more money a person has, the more energy that is appropriated to this particular feeling. This can drain an individual and drain him until eventually he does not have any energy left.

Our basic purpose on earth is to advance. Civilizations help people advance. People start out as a family unit and move to a tribe. Then a tribe becomes a community. The community can develop into a society and the society can become a civilization. This is the natural order of things. This natural order is followed regardless of where people are in the world. But it can be interrupted and stopped anywhere along the line.

If a group is intelligent enough that they adhere to the natural laws and advance to the point that they become a civilization, a synergy takes place. The whole becomes greater than the sum of its parts. This is what The Angel of North America means when she says that our society is on the verge of taking a step and becoming a civilization. But we are not there. Evil is working as hard as it can to prevent us from evolving into a civilization. Evil starts with a breakdown of the family. We have such a breakdown.

Let me give you the benefit of The Teacher's perspective on our history in this regard. First, we went through the tribal stage where families and groups joined together for the common good. This was true before the Civil War. Even afterward this continued and society advanced. The country grew after the Civil War, coming back together after a time to advance to the level of a community. We congealed into a true society upon entering World War I. At the end of World War II the stage was set for our society to grow into a civilization.

Becoming a civilization does not happen over night. The Teacher says that a hundred years of struggle and turmoil, between three and four generations, is what is generally required for a human society to advance to that of a civilization. After World War II the stage was set. When a people make advances that are beyond what is known or has been accomplished before, they can move from being a society to the level of a civilization.

Two steps have been taken so far that qualify in The Teacher's estimation. One is the use of atomic energy and the other is the probes sent into outer space and our landings on the moon. The cumulative effects of the advancements in research and in science and technology are what lift humans from a society to a civilization. But our momentum has stopped. A whole generation has passed since we made that last big step. People have turned inward and yet there has been no spiritual awakening.

A leader came before momentum was lost, a Yogi known as the Marhareshee Yogi. He offered spiritual guidance. At the same time people were moving to higher and higher technological levels. The Teacher tells us that if people had embraced that spiritual guidance at the same time we were progressing technologically, we would still be moving with momentum toward becoming a civilization. But we did not.

Advancing into a civilization does not happen with a single isolated step. In the past, civilizations have been marked by great building efforts. We have the saying, "Rome wasn't built in a day." Civilizations have been marked by colonizations. Colonizations led to assimilations of diverse peoples. The information that was shared by people when they came together under the guidance and the laws and the collective consciousness of a society produced something greater than they had had as separate peoples. What happened was more than a natural progression. It was a leap forward.

Rome was a society for approximately 400 years before it took the leap. There was a progression of pagan leaders. Some were ruthless. Some were kind. But none had the combination of the will of the people and the technology to take the society ahead into a civilization. In all times and in all stages of life, humans have to obey the same laws of nature as all other creatures. But when the technology and the will of the people are in harmony with the natural order, there can be a meeting of the collective mind that can propel people beyond where they are. For the leap to happen usually requires a strong and good leader. This leader becomes the voice of the people. He energizes them, units them, makes them want to move ahead and do more.

When a people become a civilization, individuals begin to do things for the common good. What seems a flow of energy is created so that art and music and education and science and philosophy expand into areas that have not been conceived of before. People cannot say why, but everyone works hard. They try to do their best. The absolute highest level of achievement becomes the goal. Mere survival is no longer the issue. Ideas flow and dreams come true.

Fulfilled dreams are what make a civilization great. Sometimes this can happen during the reign of a single monarch, but usually the transition happens over the course of several generations and there is a natural order which is followed. The society comes to a level where people feel that they can do more. Basic needs are satisfied and perhaps as a result, the questions of life and its mysteries become all important. Religion and philosophy and education combine in ways in which people come to realize what is best for them. They are able to see where they need to go. Once they make the determination and take action, the flower of their culture begins to bloom.

Liberal ideas do not cause a civilization to progress. A struggle is the impetus for growth and progress. The struggle forms the nucleus. It is the seed. Having to deal with the difficult issues of life and death and where the money should go make a civilization grow.

The Roman civilization grew out of a land that could barely support the people who lived on it. This great civilization came about because of the demand for conquest in order to satisfy the needs of the people. Rome was not built because of the democracy of the senate. Necessity built the empire. The Romans were not friendly. The Romans conquered. They took over the land and enslaved the people. The Gauls, the Saxons, Normans, Hebrews and Carthaginians whom the Romans conquered all had societies. What these peoples lacked was the determination and the will to become civilizations in their own right. The Teacher tells us that this is the natural process. Necessity and determination are the keys. This is what God intended.

There is a role for natural selection in the development of humans. Building civilizations is a way for the natural process to unfold. The Teacher tells us that the time is near for the society of the United States to evolve into a civilization. It has not happened because a national will to conquer the unknown and to accomplish more does not exist. The liberal view is too strong that everyone must be taken care of. The view exists that the nation is so wealthy that all our problems should be solved before we can go further. The Teacher says that this thinking is wrong. We are not following the natural order. For example, pockets exist where people are trying to take care of the environment. The natural order is for this to be done by the general will of the people. It should not be legislated. Laws take away from the will of the people. They inhibit free will. They stifle creativity. They hold people back.

Feelings of individual self-interest also are too strong. People are looking out only for themselves. We lack the national goal behind which all can unite. Nevertheless, the time is right. The technology is available to satisfy almost everyone's needs. What we need is a focal point, a nucleus around which we can unite. We need a strong leader who can bring a vision to the people. Until these come together the society will not be able to progress.

If we do not progress from here, history will record the United States as having been a wealthy society, one which made numerous attempts at world order but one which was lacking in any major achievement. Our society has not built anything to last. Throughout Europe, there are roads that the Romans built 2000 years ago. Structures and art from their cities have lasted more than a millennium and a half. Nothing we have built will withstand 2000 years of earthquake, flood and war.

The Romans did not have modern machines. They had nowhere near the technology we enjoy. They did not have the wealth we have today. Why, The Teacher wonders, are we so shortsighted today?

In Roman times people were able to build on what generations before them had accomplished. It was not uncommon for families to be in the same business or line of work for three or four hundred years. Ten generations could occupy the same dwellings. There was a sense of family. None of this exists in today's society.

Cities are not built with families in mind. They are built for maximum exploitation. People who own buildings seldom if ever live or work in them.

Transportation and communication take such enormous percentages of society's wealth. Viewed from where The Teacher sits, she has to ask, what sense does this make? Cities should not become so large that they outstrip the ability of an area to feed them. This is against the natural order. People should not become so concerned with long distance communication that they do not even know their neighbors. How can a society progress when one of the chief functions of the government is to sort out who is at fault for everything that happens in the daily lives of individuals? These are not things that help nurture a civilization.

When Rome was building its empire huge taxes were extracted from conquered peoples. These monies, the goods and the fruits of these labors, were sent back to build a great city. Rome did not tax its own. It did not accrue a huge national debt. In the building process it did not incur huge costs for future generations to pay. Our society has gone from an era of building to an era of decline and there has been no building of a civilization in between.

The liberal views that are so rampant in our society are

all indications of a society in decline. Consider for example the mess we have created with our welfare state, the excessive taxes we put on the people, our huge and bloated government, that people are no longer willing to take responsibility for their own lives, that we have no common religion, that people do not want to do any more than what they absolutely have to, our excessive concern with drugs, rampant homosexuality and the state of medical treatment for the elderly.

When was our Golden Age? Some people say it is yet to come. But how can it come when the system will be bankrupt? The Teacher tells us that first a society becomes morally bankrupt by not having a firm and established religion. The breakdown of family units follow. Not only do we have unwed mothers, but we often have two generations of unwed mothers under one roof. Another sign of breakdown is not being able to supply meaningful work for all the people.

Unfortunately, the biggest source of our problem is our government. In terms of world history, the society of the United States has the opportunity to be the best civilization the world has ever known. Ours is supposed to be a government of the people, but it is not. The technology now exists for us to have a more representative form of government. By this The Teacher does not mean sending more representatives to Washington. Why is it, she asks, that a news service can take a poll and find that 76% of the people believe that taxes are too high, yet the elected representatives who should be listening to these people do nothing to lower taxes?

If the national consensus or will of the people is that taxes are too high, then taxes should be be lowered. The simple fact is that if that means cutting welfare payments then welfare payments should be cut. If it means not building an airplane that costs a figure equal to the entire budget of a small state, the airplane should not be built.

Our representative form of government must have a national mind. It should not have hundreds of individual minds, each with its own particular self-interest to protect. When Rome was being built, senators argued the politics, but a leader made the decisions where to send the army. A leader decided what monuments to build and what new lands to conquer. At the end of the twentieth century the new lands to conquer are well outside the confines of national borders. The scope must be bigger than anything anyone may be able to imagine at this time.

Some believe that using money to conquer space is foolish and wasteful when so many problems remain to be solved on every block in every city of our country. But solving the problem of every individual would be to take responsibility away from the very people we would be trying to help. There can be no doubt that it would interfere with their free will. In addition, using our resources in this way rather than to conquer space is robbing people of a dream they might otherwise experience.

The history of the world is dotted with people who had what others believed were unrealistic dreams. Such dreams are a recurring characteristic of the history of civilizations. Whenever something great was achieved people first had to go beyond what they already knew in search of something better. The Teacher assures us that something better is out there. We need to find it. The answers to our questions lie just beyond our view. There is no longer any purpose served in redrawing lines on the globe. This has already been done too many times. We need to go beyond. Space is what we need to conquer.

God's plan is for people on earth to evolve to the highest form possible. His plan is for us to use technology to free ourselves from what keeps us here on earth. His plan is for us to use our intellect to grow and to develop into beings of a higher order than we are today. God wants us to use our wills and our talents along with technology to defeat evil and to achieve an end to our world before he decides that the time has come for him to end it.

The Teacher says that in God's plan the end of the world will come when all of the spirits have had an opportunity, a fair and just opportunity, to choose between good and evil. If evil can be defeated, human life on earth will end because there will be no more purpose for it being here.

Earth is the interface between good and evil. We are here to have an opportunity of trial, an opportunity to use our free will to combat the forces and temptations of evil. God's hope is that all people will overcome the temptations and choose him. He wants every spirit to return to him. But God knows that not every spirit will. As people progress they have continual opportunities by means of reincarnation[1] and the recycling of souls. This recycling of souls keeps the collective human spirit alive and moving forward so that every soul can help advance the evolution of mankind. In this way every soul has an opportunity to bring more of a God-like spirit to the collective consciousness of humanity.

Whether or not you wish to believe it, The Teacher assures us that the notion of wanting to do better, the notion of wanting to have more than just an existence,

---

[1]   Many Christians will have difficulty with the idea of reincarnation since this generally is not one of the accepted doctrines of the Church. Some scholars believe that during the fourth and fifth centuries when the cannon was formalized, the concept was judged to be counterproductive. It was thought that some potential converts would put off their acceptance of Christ believing they would have chances in future lives to do so. Reincarnation was eliminated as a result. Close scrutiny of the Bible will reveal, however, what Jesus and his disciples actually thought. Consider Matthew 16:13-14. According to it, many people of the day believed Jesus was Elijah or Jeremiah or one of the other prophets. Presumably this would have to have happened as a result of reincarnation since the last prophet of the Old Testament lived some 400 years before Christ. Jesus himself proclaimed John the Baptist to have been Elijah in Matthew 11:14. He is quoted as having said, "And if you will believe it, he [John the Baptist] is the Elijah who was to come." Also, consider the story of Jesus healing the blind man as recounted in John 9:1-12, which begins, "As he went along, he saw a man blind from birth. His disciples asked him, 'Rabbi, who sinned, this man or his parents, that he was born blind?'"

Since the man was blind from birth, the only way his own sins could have caused his blindness was for him to have sinned in a former life. Jesus did not tell his followers this wasn't possible. To the contrary, he seems to have assumed it was, although he gives another reason for the man's blindness.

—Editor

the notion of heaven and a life beyond this world all come from the collective consciousness that we call God. She tells us that in a sense all people are God. He is in each one of us and each one of us is a part of him. God is the longing and yearning to do more which keeps goodness alive on earth.

But simply keeping goodness alive is not enough. Eventually we must defeat evil. The quintessential way would be for us to use technology to free ourselves; to use our mental capacity to become purely spiritual beings. In effect we would become angels. The Teacher says this can happen without our having to die. When we defeat evil on earth we will be free to become more than we are now. People will leave the earth willingly to become part of the energy flow.

If humans leave the earth in this way the species of animals that are left on earth including fish and insects will remain and continue to develop and evolve as humans did after the age of reptiles. The spirits that now live in human bodies all will have either gone to heaven or to hell and there will be no need for a cataclysmic end of the world. There will be no need for a final judgment. All of the spirits will have had an opportunity to choose for themselves. They will have chosen either heaven or hell. The world will once again become a neutral place, devoid of good or evil.

But God will intervene if mankind does not develop and use technology to become spiritual beings. He will intervene if the force of evil becomes so strong that the balance is tipped irrevocably in favor of evil. The Teacher reminds us repeatedly that God will not allow the spirits he has created to be subject to pressures so great that they cannot employ free will. Rather, he will end the lesson of mankind and make a judgment on the spot of who will pass into heaven and who will be damned forever without his love and energy. This judgment will be a time of great sorrow, suffering and pain. But it will be necessary to save those who are good and want to choose God.

Whether we humans leave the earth of our own volition or as the result of a final judgment, the world will not necessarily end as a globe in space where life exists. The world may simply be left without humans. We are told, however, that a hundred million years could pass before a species may once again develop to the point where it can be a vehicle for souls.

This is the overall plan of God for earth and mankind as related to me by his messenger, The Angel of North America.

GOOD AND EVIL

The Teacher explained that God does not punish individuals, nor does he wish to punish whole societies. He will send a punishment, however, when one becomes necessary to restore the balance of good and evil. This is the state our society now is entering. We are teetering on the brink of a catastrophe of unimaginable proportions. The reason is quite clear. Evil is close to achieving the upper hand.

The purpose of evil is to drain free will from souls and to destroy man's connection to God. Through life in human form, God has given us a challenge to use our talents to build and to grow. Evil seeks to destroy this. People build their societies with talents given by God. The building of a society is a quest to achieve a higher order of actualization. It is a quest to go beyond the satisfaction of the needs of food, shelter and clothing in order to achieve an understanding of the meaning of life. Evil wants to tear this down. Evil does not want people to understand how to get to heaven. Evil's only dominion is on earth. This is the only place that evil exists. Outside of earth, evil is a void, an emptiness that will never experience the energy of God. Once all the people on earth recognize this and have an understanding that they have a higher purpose, once they understand that their souls can be released and go on to be part of the cosmic energy that is God, the world will come to an end and evil will no longer exist. Therefore, evil is fighting for its survival.

What we will call evil in this book is the force that takes away free will. This is what the dark side wishes. This taking of free will and ultimately of souls is how the force of darkness energizes itself.

A punishment is visited upon a society when the force of evil or darkness has gotten the upper hand. It happens when a society has become so corrupt that freedom of choice, the freedom to choose God freely or not to choose God, has become so difficult that people do not have a fair chance to save their souls. We are approaching this state in our society today. A punishment to correct this will occur when the pole shift comes, unless first we correct the balance of good and evil. If we can do so, our society will pull together and overcome the hardships brought on by the earth changes. We will emerge stronger and wiser and ready to move on to a higher level of actualization.

I have been asked why the struggle between good and evil has not been the topic of books in recent years which have come to us from spirit entities or angels. People have mentioned *Mary's Message to the World*. They have talked about *A Course in Miracles*. Some have pointed to the series by Kryon. I have not read any of these books because I have been instructed not to do so by The Teacher. She does not want my thinking to be influenced. Whether or not these messages are correct I do not know. As a result of my restricted reading on the subject, I can write only what I have been told by The Teacher. This is how she wants it. What I do know is that the message I bring is what is needed at this time. Of this, I am absolutely certain.

Until now in modern times there has been no reason to talk about the struggle of good and evil. The Teacher assures me that God does not want to interfere in our lives. To send a message is to risk doing so. Free choice is of paramount concern. God does not want us to base our actions on the fear of retribution. He would rather for us to choose him because choosing him is what we wish of our own free will. Once the scales have tipped toward evil, however, the physical realm we live in no longer provides a fair opportunity to choose freely. A punishment's purpose is not to punish per se, but to set the balance right. It is necessary for enough of the evil to be wiped out so that a new society may begin with a fresh slate. In this way a new environment will have been created in which spirits in human bodies can freely choose God or not choose God.

God does not want to send a punishment. Much suffering will occur. Good people as well as evil ones will die. We have come a long way in North America and are in a position to create a magnificent culture if only we can muster the will. A punishment will mean that much time will be lost in humanity's growth toward what can be a new and enlightened reality.

Ultimately, evil will be conquered because it will no longer be necessary. A punishment will only delay this golden era. This is why God is sending this message now through his angels. This is why The Angel of North America has come to me and asked me to write this book. We as a society are being given the opportunity to restore the balance of good and evil before God steps in and does it for us.

The meaning of life is to save your soul. It is a question of God, of faith, and of humanity. If you believe in God as the Creator of all things, you have the faith to believe in something that you cannot see or touch or smell. You should have a belief that man was created in God's image, that humanity has value and purpose and is sacred. It is your job to protect and to preserve and to nurture this belief.

Everyone has a soul until they lose it or give it away. "Losing your soul" is a figure of speech. One doesn't really "lose" their soul. A soul is eternal, part of the universal consciousness for all time, but it can be drained of God's energy or given over to evil for any number of reasons. In this sense, the soul is lost. Being drained prevents the spirit from being in God's energy and love.

The soul is how God touches us in our daily lives. It is the part of our being that connects us to the universal consciousness and the energy we call God. It is the part of us that God does not directly control. It is the ticket we have punched to enter heaven, or to trade in exchange for worldly pleasures. You can lose your soul, sell it, or give it away. However this happens a person is left with a tremendously empty feeling, a feeling that cannot be satisfied. No amount of money, no amount of power, fame, position or sex can fill the void one feels when they have cut themselves off from God. The shock of not feeling God, of having love drained away, the loneliness, can drive people mad. People often kill themselves when they realize what they have done. This is sad, but we see it happen everyday. It could be happening to you right now. Beyond trying to head off the impending punishment and explaining that good and evil have gotten out of balance, I was told to write this book to restore the knowledge in each one of us that **the meaning of life is to save our souls.** The force of evil in our society has become too great and this is making the task far too difficult.

By what means can a soul be lost?

You can lose your soul to temptation and buy a one-way ticket to hell by giving in to vices. These are pleasures in excess or those that hurt your body. Little by little your strength of will is compromised. You become spiritually weakened. Little by little you lose part of your soul. This is the test of daily life we all must endure. Even so, life can be very good. It can be pleasurable. It can be the best way to achieve eternal happiness.

You can lose your soul to Evil when you do not use your free will to make decisions. Giving up your will to another, such as your boss, a political leader, an organization, or even your mother can cause you to lose your soul. This is the gradual way. You lose your soul a little at a time. You may not even realize the problem until one day you find that you are unhappy and have been for some time. No diet, no food, clothes or vacation, no job or activity will make you happy. The best you can achieve is distraction. And no distraction will last.

As long as you do not die in this state, however, God can replace and replenish your soul. But you must repent. You must be sorry for what you have done. You must have learned enough not to do it again. Only then will love and satisfaction come back into you life.

Finally, you can make a deal with the devil and sell your soul. This is not to be taken lightly. It is a most serious offense against God. It is also a serious offense against your fellow human beings as well as yourself.

The devil is always waiting for you to slip and to say, "I'd give anything for—" When you do, he'll be right there. The best deals he makes are with young people. A soul can be purchased for inexpensive jewelry, a date with the right person, concert tickets. People ask why a teenager has no joy in his life. What could possibly be so bad he would kill himself? The answer may be he had joy taken from him because of his own folly.

How many sociologists or counselors have asked about peer pressure or lack of self-esteem or drug use and have never even considered the overwhelming loneliness, the complete emptiness, the loss of love for self that is the direct result of selling one's soul? How many of us take the time to talk with our children and to tell them about the meaning of life?

The meaning of life is to save your soul. It is the

reason we are here on earth.

Many in our society do not accept that evil is a force, that evil is real, and that its purpose is to control lives. In and of itself, evil is powerless. It simply exists. It does not destroy. It does not grow of its own accord. It is passive. It is in the exercise of free will that evil grows. Temptation is the catalyst. Evil uses temptation to induce people to accept evil and to allow it to work through them. What people call sin is the accepting of evil. The act of sinning, doing the wrong thing, allows evil into you.

Imagine the soul as a vessel, a cup. Choosing sin, going against your conscience, removes some of the goodness, the energy, the life force from the cup. It allows evil in. The more frequently people give into the evil, the faster their cup will be drained. Eventually, the person will be empty. This emptiness results in the despair described earlier. The soul yearns for goodness. It yearns to be filled with the energy of life, the energy of God.

Evil seeks to maintain the emptiness, for emptiness is the essence of evil.

Here is an example. People who take drugs are doing something wrong. Just the act of using drugs is bad. They know it, but after a while they feel powerless to stop. They feel good while they are taking the drugs because they are making decisions. They can keep making the decisions until their soul is completely drained. Then there is nowhere left to go. They have no more reasonable choices, no more options or decisions left they can make in their lives. Now evil controls them. They have hit what is known as "rock bottom." They feel totally helpless. Nothing satisfies them but they continue taking the drug. Evil has taken over. The soul is empty.

It will not be enough for that person to rehabilitate. It will not be enough to get them to stop taking the drug. An emptiness exists in their life that goes beyond comprehension. Evil has accomplished its goal of taking all that person's strength. It will use that empty vessel in its search for new energy. It will reach out and drain those closest to the one whose soul is lost. This state is beyond human intervention.

Is there any way for the soul of this person to be refilled? Yes. The person must first recognize that evil has taken them over. They must ask God for help. Then they must fight the evil, pray, and do good works.

This sounds easy. It is very difficult. Evil in this situation is extremely strong. Nearly superhuman strength will be required. It may sound trivial but it is true, only God can help in a situation like this. The free will to choose between right and wrong is the most powerful force in the universe. In every sense it is a struggle of biblical proportions. Few people can overcome evil that has taken their soul.

It is a life-long struggle not to give into temptation, not to do bad things. I am not speaking of eating too much fat in one's diet or smoking cigarettes. It is not a sin, for instance, to go through a stop sign. It is against the law. It is not right. It is one of man's laws that help the society to run. The law is necessary, but breaking it is not a sin.

This is one reason man needs to be careful not to make too many laws. In the struggle to regain one's soul a person must be aware of right and wrong and always do what is right. Doing what is right rebuilds strength. Rebuilding strength gives energy to fight evil. Fighting evil refills the soul. At last when the soul is full, goodness spills out and a person naturally begins doing good works for others. This is the state we all should strive for.

How difficult is it to be like this? Extremely. In all of human history only Jesus was able to do it his entire life. Everyone else has to settle for less than perfection because they are human. But it is the struggle that leads to the reward. It is through the struggle that you will earn a place in heaven.

What is the difference between right and wrong and good an evil?

Good and evil are forces in the universe that are outside the control of man. The decision between right and wrong is always within man's control. People cannot control evil. They can only fight it.

Good is the life force that flows into them when they fight evil, do good works and pray to or praise God. It is the strength behind a person's conscience that gives them the knowledge and the understanding to make the right decisions.

Life is a path you are on. Only one reason exists for going down the path. This is to save your soul. It is not to make money. It is not to save the world, find a cure for cancer, or write the best song or novel. Those may be things you do while on your path. You may get married. You may have children. You may enjoy the trip. But at the end, if your soul isn't intact, your life will have had no meaning. Its purpose will have been missed. Why? **The meaning of life is to save your soul.**

Why are people today seeking spiritual answers more than ever before in modern times? Because evil is so prevalent in this society. People keep asking, "Why is this happening? Why are things so bad?" They refuse to accept that evil is taking over.

Evil is controlling us in many ways: Through man's laws, through taxes, advertising, greed, power, and through a lack of faith and the refusal of many to accept God in their lives.

Life does not come easy. Everything that you achieve in life must be earned. You have trials which you must overcome in order to demonstrate effort. Some people have more than others. I have not been told why.

Some are born with trials. Others are given trials. Some take on trials because of choices they make in this life. Trials are obstacles that must be overcome. Having an abnormal child is a trial. Being born with a disability and having to learn to live with it is another. A trial is having to recover from having chosen the wrong mate.

How are trials overcome? By accepting what God has given. By using the talents that God has given you in order to compensate for the difficulty. By asking God for help and the strength not to give up. By not letting others make decisions for you and thereby giving up your free will.

Having trials in your life can build strength. But trials can drain you if you do not accept and decide to overcome them.

Trials come in many, many forms. It can be a trial to be born poor and have to struggle for life. It can be a trial to be born rich and have to struggle for salvation. No one is immune and no one can buy his way out of the trials he must overcome.

The ability to buy one's way out of difficulty represents a strong temptation in our society. People buy their way out of having to care for their children. They buy their way out of having to care for family members. By donating money, they buy their way out of doing good deeds for others.

Some may try to buy their way out of their trials by attempting foolish deeds, perhaps by seeking fame and publicity. One form of foolishness might be devoting one's life to an obscure sport because of a disability. Another is putting one's life at risk by climbing a mountain or walking a tight rope between the towers of the World Trade Center. You are here on earth to save your soul. Acts such as these are not going to help you do it. They may end your life and thereby preclude any possibility of salvation.

Someone who shortens his life by doing something dangerous for money has wasted a very precious opportunity given by God. Is there any redemptive value, for example, in race car drivers hurling themselves around in metal boxes at hundreds of miles per hour? This is no different than the gladiators in the coliseums of Jesus' time. People go to these events expecting to see death. Without death and destruction the sport is not exciting.

The trials one has to overcome may seem unfair. They may seem to have been given out disproportionally. This is not the way to look at trials or at life. If you are able to endure your trials and overcome them, your soul will fill. The gift you have been given is the opportunity for your spirit to challenge evil, overcome it and thereby to fill your soul and have an opportunity to be with God.

Life has miracles. Life has trials. Life has mysteries. Life has holiness. Life has pain. Life will end. I can assure you that what you need to do, what you need to have happen in order to save your soul and to avert God's punishment is to overcome your trials by exercising free will to make the right choices.

Every epoch is different. Every society is different. There are prophets and teachers and guides for every time and every society, just as there are people chosen to be ready to survive God's punishments and to begin society anew. Whether or not those chosen are needed, they are always here on earth, ready and waiting.

As messengers and guides, The Angel of North America and her helpers have the task of telling people what to look for, what signs to follow in order to choose the right path in their lives. But it is up to each individual to make his own decision of what path to follow. Each of us must make his own decisions in order to save his own soul. A person cannot follow anyone else. He cannot have someone make the decisions for him. One cannot escape the responsibility. The making of a decision is the important thing.

People feel that they can escape responsibility by saying that they are doing something in the name of a corporation. This does not hold water. People who attempt to shift responsibility or to shirk it are fooling themselves.

61

The trials of life are individual responsibilities which cannot be avoided. They cannot be shifted to others. They must be overcome.

Why is it important to make decisions? It is important to fight and overcome evil, to build strength and fill one's soul. Making decisions, doing good works and praying are all interwoven into life on earth as opportunities that people have to fill their souls and gain entrance to heaven. One must make decisions in order to choose the path of his life. By not making decisions one gives over free will to others. When one "lets things happen," he gives over his will to the force of evil that is constantly waiting to drain him. Evil is always around you, like air. It is part of the human experience. Without evil one would not be alive. One would be in heaven with God. One would no longer be human. The presence of evil is the human condition. Having to fight evil is being human. Free will is the tool that God gave us to gain entrance to heaven. Free will requires decisions. Free will requires choices. Free will requires conscious thought and reflection concerning good and evil. Without consciously thinking through choices one gives up free will.

God does not want a person's free will. The devil does. The devil does in fact exist. If you simply let things happen to you, you give up free will. Evil is waiting and ready to drain you.

To make a decision is to do something positive. Even though it may not work out right, energy flows into you. Energy flowing in fills your soul. On the other hand, letting things happen, or letting time go by drains and weakens your spirit. Eventually you will end up empty, seeking to be filled, and draining others.

Here is an example. You have a sister who made a bad choice of a mate and did not do something to correct the situation. Let's call her Martha. Eventually, Martha becomes drained and miserable. She comes to you for help. Without terminating that relationship, without repenting and making a decision to go forward with her life and recover from her mistake, Martha will drain you. She will drain you and your family and make you miserable. Why? Martha has not made a decision. She is simply letting life happen. Her inaction has now brought you into the web of evil.

Here's another example. Your brother, Charles, has a job in which his immediate supervisor is a drained and evil person. The supervisor is using Charles and the situation is killing him. Rather than leave and thereby escape the power that is taking him over, Charles goes on thinking that this is a trial that he must endure.

Charles makes a good salary. The money is a temptation that keeps him under the power of evil. He allows it to keep him from making the right decision, which is to leave. Eventually, Charles becomes drained and miserable. He has no energy. He says that even though he has material wealth, his life has no meaning.

This is a serious time for Charles. His soul is empty. He is looking for excitement and is prone to do dangerous things. This is when the devil likes to take souls. Charles is so accustomed to not making decisions that he cannot make one to save his life. The devil realizes this.

Many die in these circumstances. They die from heart attacks, from unexplained accidents, or from taking foolish risks. This is the ultimate tragedy.

How does one recognize evil? Evil is a negative energy. Evil is an entity, a power, and evil can take the shape of the devil here on earth. This must be accepted as a matter of faith just as the existence of God is a matter of faith. Evil exists whether you like it or not. Even if you do not believe in evil it can affect you. One cannot be neutral. There is no safe zone.

The purpose of evil is to take your soul and to keep it from being with God. This is the struggle of the world. Evil cannot affect the natural order. The natural order has no will of its own. The natural order is God's will and cannot be defeated. Evil is only able to affect human beings because God made humans in his own image.

"In his image" means people have a spirit, that they have a soul, that they have free will. These are the components of God's image. Outward appearance is not.

This spirit recognizes goodness. The soul is the sphere of energy that holds goodness and contains the essence of a person. Free will is the ability to choose right from wrong. Good and evil are different from right and wrong. Our society has confused the meanings. People no longer understand the difference in these terms. When a person does not understand, they cannot recognize evil. Actually, it is very simple. Evil wants you to do bad things that will drain your soul. It will reward you for not following the Commandments, reward you for hurting others, and reward you for giving over your will. God does not reward you for these things.

If you are receiving rewards for doing bad things, things that are wrong, against the Commandments, you are losing your soul. Evil is taking control of you.

What is right and what is wrong? Right is following the Commandments. One must do good things for others. One must glorify God by using his talents to the best of his ability. One must glorify God through praise to him and prayer. Wrong is everything else. Wrong is being obsessed with self. Wrong is using God-given talents to hurt others. Wrong is disobeying the Commandments. Wrong is giving one's will over to others so that others control them.

The central focus of evil is control over a person's free will. If you feel as though you are being controlled, chances are evil is working on you. The naysayers of our society would like you to believe that everyone is controlled. This is partly true in that evil is so powerful today in North

America. This is why the angels came to my husband and me. They came to tell us that we must change.

If you wake up one morning and wonder "What is the meaning of life?" and you no longer know, your soul has been drained. There is no more meaning to your life because your soul has been sucked dry. It is empty. You have given your life away. Somewhere along the way you have made a deal with the devil and your fate will be sealed unless you act immediately to begin refilling your soul.

At the point before you die, when you feel there is nothing left to live for, you will have an opportunity to repent. But once you die with your soul empty, if you have not asked for help, your life will be over and your soul will be gone. It will be out of touch with the energy of the universe which is God and forever damned to the loneliness of hell.

Evil wants control over your mind and over your will. Evil is the force that allows crime to pay. Evil is the force that rewards bad behavior. Evil is the force that propels wrongful power to control people's lives.

Here are a few examples.

Two boys, Ralph and Henry, meet after school. They talk about stealing a car and going for a "joy ride." The mere fact that the idea comes into being is from the force of evil. Ralph and Henry discuss it. They argue for and against stealing the car, but in the end they decide to steal it. They have given into evil.

Ralph and Henry steal the car and have fun. They take the car for a few miles to a shopping center. They leave the car and go to discuss what they have done. It has been an exhilarating and exciting experience. They did not get caught. They had a good time. Evil has rewarded them. Unless Ralph and Henry have been taught that this is wrong behavior, no reason exists in their minds why they should not do it again.

The laws in our society today do not fight evil. They often are made to fight the effects of evil but not the source. This is why evil has been able to grow so strong.

Here is another example. A person works in the bank, has done a good job and is moved up to the position of branch manager. We will call him William. William now feels caught in the middle. He knows that his superiors sometimes ask him to do things that are wrong such as back-dating documents, refusing loans for arbitrary reasons, cheating on time cards of employees. William is concerned by this, but there is no one to report this to because it is an unwritten policy that people do whatever they are told.

William knows in his heart that what he is doing is wrong. If he continues these actions, he will lose part of his soul with each wrongful act. As time passes William no longer feels that these things are wrong. At the point his conscience no longer bothers him, evil is in control.

As another example, let's consider the case of Harriet, a school administrator. Harriet has just been promoted to assistant superintendent and needs to find someone to fill her old position. After a few weeks Harriet learns that the new person is doing a better job than she had done. Harriet becomes jealous. Eventually, Harriet lets the jealousy consume her. She gives in to the temptation of self-pride and does everything within her power to make the new person look bad. Harriet does not want the newcomer doing a better job than she had done. Harriet uses her power to hurt, to tear her down, to make the new person's life miserable. Harriet misleads her colleagues and lies about what she has done.

Harriet is letting the temptation of evil control her by hurting another. When a person no longer has a conscience, when she begins believing her own lies, when she works at destroying another's reputation to make herself look good, she has let evil take control of her soul.

She will wake up one morning and find that nothing makes her happy any longer. The only thing that seems to satisfy her is hurting others. This becomes a way of life. She no longer is able to recognize what she is doing. Her soul has been drained. She has given it over to evil.

It is not easy to know when you are being drained. Others close to you will recognize it before you do. If you had made an outright deal with the devil you would know it. But few people actually make such a deal. Most lose their souls by giving into temptation a little at a time. They begin by justifying things they know are wrong. After a while they do not worry about it anymore. It becomes a part of their life. They begin to lie, to cheat, to deceive people and it does not bother them. They do not even think about it on a conscious level. It becomes so much a part of their life, a part of their business, a part of their personality that it becomes part of them. Their friends will change. They may recognize in their friends that they are caught up in a life of one-upmanship, a life of keeping up with the Joneses. They are never satisfied. Nothing seems to be enough. They are never happy.

At this stage people become desperate. Real crime takes place. They have the attitude that it does not matter who they have to walk over. It does not matter who they have to hurt. They begin to think that they deserve the excess they get and that others are jealous of them, perhaps standing in the way of their goal. A person given over to evil such as this cannot stop until they have it all. Yet there is no satisfaction. Eventually there is nothing else to achieve, nothing new to acquire. No one else exists they can control or hurt. Nothing is left in their life but emptiness. They are close to the end. By this time they are completely drained.

Two courses of action usually are left at this point. The devil can use this individual to gain control over others, or the person begins considering suicide.

If you are thinking about suicide you have arrived at the cusp of evil's ultimate goal, which is to take your soul. Your free will has been controlled for so long that it may no longer exist. You may go into a depression so deep that you may kill yourself. If you do, the devil has won. He has gotten your soul and left your family devastated.

The progression that led to this began with giving into temptation. It may have been a few drinks. It may have started with taking a job for more money. It may have been driving too fast. It could have been stealing, usually something small. Perhaps you took a job as a supervisor that you were not ready for. You enjoyed the feeling of power and of having control over others.

Thousands of temptations exist. Sex is a temptation. Too often in our society children begin experimenting with it before they are ready. Too much freedom compounds the situation. For a young person to be able to do what they want and not have to think about others creates conditions for giving in without thinking twice. There is the temptation of self-pride which may lead to spending too much on clothes, cosmetics or jewelry. Temptations abound.

Let us consider an average person, say, for example, Sally, a secretary for a county administrator. Can evil take Sally over? Certainly, even though Sally is not seeking power. She is not seeking position. Sally knows that she is not going to get rich. Sally thinks she is leading a good Christian life. How can evil possibly affect her?

In this situation the evil may come from the top down. Sally realizes one day that since she got her new boss, she does not like coming to work. Sally thinks he is cheating in some way. Perhaps he is hurting other people and she is helping him.

Sally asks herself, should she look the other way when he takes three hour lunches? Should she help him cover up when he makes mistakes that she knows cost a lot of money?

Sally decides not to bring these things to anyone's attention. Sally lets him use her to do his personal work. Little by little she allows him to control her.

Sally's conscience bothers her but she justifies her actions by saying that she needs her job. Sally overrides her conscience by saying that there is a greater good, that she has to work in order to take care of her family.

The fact is, when a person does not fight evil it drains them. It drains them little by little until they feel so bad about themselves that they do not like the person they have become.

This situation is all the more difficult because if Sally gives over to evil she will be rewarded. How? Her boss will start giving her afternoons off with pay. Sally knows this is wrong but does it. She may get a bigger title, say to "executive assistant," and a raise to go with it. She might get new office equipment before anyone else. Her boss may offer new responsibilities that put her in control of others.

At first Sally asks herself what she did to deserve this. She may tell herself she is not ready. She cannot handle it yet. But then, Sally takes what is offered.

Sally has given over to evil and has been rewarded.

Evil works by giving immediate gratification, positive and substantial rewards related directly to your actions. This is how it works, but you do not feel good about it. You have to talk yourself into believing you deserve what you get. If you find yourself doing this, beware that you are headed down the wrong path. You have to fight evil every step of the way.

Life is difficult. God does not reward every good deed immediately. Nevertheless, when you are on the right path and get a promotion you deserve there is a feeling of satisfaction and of having the strength to be able to do the job. You rise to the task and find it enjoyable. On the other hand, if you give into evil and allow your boss to control you, you will feel drained. The constant fight with your conscience will keep you from being happy. You will feel tense. You may be curt with family members. You will not be happy about your work. You will find ways to avoid it. Your health will be affected. This is evil draining you. Even if you do not give in to evil, it will drain you and drain you, until you become depressed. You will have a feeling of worthlessness, of emptiness, of sadness. Nothing will satisfy you until you get away from this job.

Perhaps you decide you need a vacation. After a week you feel happy. Life has meaning again. Your children are wonderful. The grass looks green. But you absolutely cannot stand the thought of going back to the office.

This is not some abstract pressure you wish to avoid. It is not a personality conflict. It has nothing to do with psychobabble about personality disorders. It is purely and simply evil. Evil is what you cannot stand, what you do not want to be subjected to. It is an invisible but very real force that is draining you. You must face the reality of evil and get out of that job.

Evil is a force that is bigger than any human. It is more powerful than most of us can understand. On earth evil is equal to the power of good, or what most would think of as God or love.

God has dominion over all things and God is more powerful than evil. But on earth, in human terms, good and evil are equal forces. The struggle of good and evil has been written about and discussed and brought out in the human drama throughout the ages. In modern times people often seem to view evil as superstition. Modern people do not want to be superstitious because this indicates a lack of knowledge and understanding. So they dismiss evil.

The Teacher tells us that "modern times" come and go. There have always been times of golden age and renaissance. There have always been ages of new knowledge. There have been flowerings of the human spirit throughout the history of mankind. These flowerings are the periods of peace and tranquility. They are the periods of spiritual rebirth people have after a punishment has cleansed their societies. These periods never last because as soon as people lose the fear of evil, evil begins again to gain control of a society.

Humans have an unlimited capacity for love and understanding but a low tolerance for evil, for resisting the temptations of greed, of power, of lying and adultery. When one gives in to temptations such as these they are rewarded quickly and well. The rewards of pleasure, material goods, and the exhilaration of power induce people to give over their free will to the evil force.

How does one give over? It happens when a person disobeys the basic Commandments. When a person is small and goes into a store and steals a candy bar and no one corrects him, when there is no parent to point out that what they have done was wrong, the child immediately will get gratification from eating the candy. He may even be rewarded through the respect of his peers because he got away with stealing and thereby beat the system. Once a child is given a positive reinforcement for doing wrong, the force of evil begins to take over. The lack of information and understanding that this is wrong removes strength from the soul. It weakens free will.

A person's free will is that part of them that is their conscience. It is the collective reasoning of the society that informs an individual what to choose. Making the correct choice is always difficult for small children. Making the wrong choice is always easier. As people mature and grow into adolescence and adulthood, a firm direction is established in a person. If there is positive direction from the society at large it will become easier to make the right choices. This is the way it should be. When faced with choices involving religion, politics, and societal issues, the choice to do wrong should become increasingly difficult with age. By mid life people should no longer question what is right and what is wrong. They should be in possession of good values. They should have become strong. They should set positive examples to their young. This is how a society progresses in the correct way.

This progression requires an understanding of God and of the reason we are here on earth. It requires an understanding of evil and of the meaning of life. It requires close knit families and a sense of community and faith. Among peers there must be an understanding of where society has come from and where it is going. There needs to be common beliefs and a shared experience in order for people to develop the trust and faith that all understand what is good and that all are striving to achieve God's love and acceptance.

I say God's love and acceptance because of our notion of judgment. God loves and accepts everyone. It is up to the individual to make a choice whether not not he loves and accepts God. People are judged to be sent to hell not because God says they are unworthy. This happens because a person did not do what was necessary on earth to make himself worthy. The basis for being worthy is the rejection of evil. People must make a conscious and prolonged effort at it.

People are born into the world innocent. Everyone is equal. No one has more understanding of good or of evil or of God or of anything else. It is up to the society in which a person is born to make the rules and to set the direction for its children. The Teacher tells us that if a society decided that Mickey Mouse or Donald Duck was the the image of God, then it would be true and correct for members of that society to worship the cartoon mouse or the cartoon duck. People should not judge other societies on how they live their lives. If the people of a society accept what they are doing to be right and true, then it is right and true for that society.

Our society is historically a Christian society. Jesus came to the earth to give people new rules and a new direction and a new way to understand God and his plan for us. Once you are armed with this information and have these facts, it is your responsibility to act on them. You can no longer say you are unaware and therefore be excused from doing what is right. It is your responsibility to seek truth in the decisions that you make and to choose wisely what is necessary to achieve your goals.

Your goals should be to live a good life, to share with others the understanding that you have achieved, and to leave this earth with your soul intact and full of God's love and energy.

Additionally, everyone should work together to have a goal for society. There is a view that having a diversified society is a worthy goal. Nothing could be further from the truth. A society should not be diverse. According to The Teacher, the definition of a society is that it is a group of people with a common experience and a common understanding. Having a common experience and understanding makes people want to work toward the same goals. In order for a society to work, people not only must have an understanding of what is good, they also must have an understanding of what is bad. When the society rejects what is bad, it fights evil. Once we regain this concept and put it into practice, our society will be in a position to withstand the coming earth changes.

It is true that a group of people can fight collective evil. The problem with our society in North America is that the fight against evil has degenerated into a myriad of specific laws. Lawyers and others in charge of producing laws seek to limit evil in tiny bits. They make little rules and regulations for people to follow in the attempt to take care of the little things and thereby solve the big problems. This will not work. People are too complex. A society is a collection of all it members. It cannot be strong on its own. The strength must come from within. It must work to exercise the free will of all its members in order to grow strong.

A concept exists among some that laws can build a protective coating around the society and that if this shell is made thick enough, evil can be held on the outside. What happens instead is that the members of the society give up their free will in order to hide behind a shell of laws. No internal strength exists to keep that shell rigid and hard and strong. Laws are insufficient to combat the evil that is constantly trying to eat away at that shell.

The society must be a muscle with a tough skin. It must be skin that is flexible enough to grow. The muscle must be exercised and used. It must be tough enough to withstand changing conditions. This toughness can only come through the members of society working as a unit to determine what is good and right for the group. The muscle of our society today has been weakened by the concept of individual rights. It is being weakened by the acceptance of unproductive activities. It is being weakened by our placing such a high value on diversity that a sense of unity has been lost. It has been weakened by the belief that society does not have to be of one mind and of one goal in order to grow and to survive. This is why we are vulnerable to anarchy and civil war when times become difficult and resources become scarce.

God has watched and directed and guided his people throughout history, constantly giving them free choice, only interfering when that balance of choice is unequal. The time for God to interfere in our society is near. Evil has taken over too much of our consciousness. God will interfere by sending a punishment to set the balance right. This is an understanding that has been with man since the beginning. It is one of the covenants God made with people in order to be a fair and a right and a just God.

GOOD AND EVIL

People in society today have some very liberal images of God. They think that God is too good and too merciful and too loving to punish us. They feel that all they have to do is to believe in God and they will be saved. They are fooling themselves.

God does not send a punishment out of spite or revenge. A punishment comes because the direction that people are taking is counter to his plan. The purpose is to bring things back into equilibrium. It is right and correct to fear this. There is pain. There is suffering. There is judgment. Those who die have to face a decision whether or not they are ready to face judgment or to try again. Once a society slips to the point where God sends messages like the one in this book, a message to all that a punishment is imminent, the direction that the society has taken has gone far in the wrong direction. This is what I have been told by The Angel of North America, a messenger of God.

TAPPING INTO GOD'S ENERGY

Praying is getting in touch with the energy that comes from God. The Teacher tells us this because, as she says, "You have to know where you are going in order to get there." Prayer is not necessarily something everyone can do right off the bat. Praying takes practice. It takes a belief in something that you cannot see and cannot feel and, in truth, is not of this earth.

There are two types of prayer. One is praying in groups. The other is praying alone. A person will receive the same feeling in either case even though the two types of prayer are different. Evil has different manifestations. So does prayer and goodness.

Group prayer is the easier of the two because the energy of God comes to the group. Participants will be bathed in it. Perhaps you have never been to a revival or to a good church or to a gathering of holy people such as a special mass by the Pope or a baptism or a confirmation. All religions have these kinds of events. Go to one and sense the goodness and energy simply by being there. You do not have to know the precise words. You do not even have to participate. If you believe, the energy will come to you. Even as a disbeliever you will be able to feel the energy around you. This energy is a powerful, moving and vibrant force that will make you want to be a part of the group. The energy brings the people in the group together and renews them. This is characteristic of prayer in a group.

Praying alone is more difficult at first. You must believe. You must clear your mind of thoughts of yourself, of others, of possessions and position. One way to clear your mind may be to recite common prayers. People who meditate, which is another word for virtually the same thing, often have a mantra. This is a sound or a word they say over and over to clear their minds. Once your mind is clear, think of raising yourself above your body. Lift yourself up. Think of getting in touch with your soul. Ask God to allow you to be a part of him.

You may speak to yourself in this state. You may speak to God or to a saint or holy person or prophet. Some like to think of deceased relatives whom they believe to be in heaven. Simply talk to them as if they were sitting next to you. You can talk about clouds. You can talk about your life, your children, your wife or your husband. Do not ask for anything at first. Rather, simply be thankful for all you have. This is how to get started. The rest you will know when it happens. You may sense voices talking back to you. You may feel little tingles of excitement even though no one else is around. In this way you will know that you are in touch.

After some practice it will become easier to feel good about saying what is on your mind. It will feel good to clear your mind through prayer in this way. When you have reached the state of clarity, begin to listen to the voices talking back to you. These voices are not in your head, they are in your soul. When you can feel this communication anytime just by asking for it, you will know that you are practicing good prayer.

The Teacher wants me to warn readers about something. When you pray well, it will change your life. You must be ready for this.

77

How will your life change? If you have not prayed before, the chances are that you have not been a particularly good person. If this is the case pay careful attention to this warning. You will find that being a good person is difficult. Others will begin to act differently toward you. Those who are closest to you will begin to mistrust you. You will lose all of your old friends. Even family members may distance themselves from you. You will feel a need to go back to certain points in your life to correct mistakes. This is called repentance. It is both necessary and good.

After repentance, you will feel as though a weight has been lifted from you. You will not want to go back to being the way you were. You will make new friends. You will see your life differently. Things will begin to look good to you no matter where you turn. You will distant yourself from bad habits and situations you may have put yourself in before. You will have a new outlook on life. One morning you will wake up and say, "How could I have ever been that other person?"

As you continue to pray and thank God for helping you and for all he has given, more and better things will come to you. But do not expect to win the lottery or to find a new car in the driveway. What will come, will come slowly. People will begin to treat you better. If you have been in a bad relationship, that will end and you will find someone who appreciates and truly loves you. You may find the strength to stop smoking. Your business may pick up because you have a different outlook. Little obstacles that once were a bother and constant irritation will go away. A state of happiness will become your norm.

Here is the bad part. You will not be able to stop talking about what you have discovered. You will want to tell every person that you see how good you feel because you have been praying. You will want them to pray too. You will feel frustrated because of all the evil in the world that people cannot see. You will not understand how others can continue doing such bad things to each other. All it takes is to ask for help and goodness will come to you.

What about people who are good and do not pray? Will they still have a difficult time?

Indeed they will. A person can do good works for others, follow the Commandments and still feel as though something is missing in his life. The missing piece is prayer. Either he has not been told the correct way to pray, or is not getting it right. Some find it easy to pray early in their life. Others spend a lifetime searching.

It helps to know that **the meaning of life is to save your soul.** Once you have this knowledge you need to know where to go for prayer. This is not a physical place. It is a state of mind. Prayer is joining with the force of energy that is God, the Universe, Love, Goodness. Some do not recognize when they have reached this place and keep looking for more. They feel that if God does not speak to them directly, they must not be praying correctly. But this simply is not true. The only sure way to have God talk to you directly is to die and go to heaven, or to be here on earth on Judgment Day.

As long as you are confined to a human body, you must accept prayer as the way you can touch the energy. You cannot be a full, living part of it. Elsa, my companion angel, tells me that she is part of the energy. She says that as a part of the energy, there is no time, there is no memory, there are none of the physical aspects of life as we know it. To be part of the energy is truly to live in the moment. It is to live the moment as eternity, the totality of time without beginning or end.

Prayer gives us a sensation of wanting to be more than we are, of wanting to be with God, of wanting to be one in spirit with God. It is the exact opposite of being drained, empty, or alone and having the thought that there is nothing left to live for. Prayer may change your life. Even so, prayer is the better way to go.

While we are on the subject of prayer let me share with you an insight about plants and their relationship to humans which has been conveyed to me by The Teacher. What do plants and prayer have in common? Each of us needs to care for plants just as each of us needs to pray regularly. Plants are our charges, our responsibility. From the rain forest to the flowers on our window sill, every single person on the planet needs to care for plants. This is important because it is how each of us truly can "get back to nature." If a person does not personally take care of a plant, he has removed himself from the flow of natural energy. This flow of natural energy is the same energy we tap into when we pray. It is the ever so delicate stream of consciousness that is the life force of all living things.

Perhaps you have difficulty growing plants. Maybe they die on you. My advice is to get a stronger plant. Get a different plant. Make your personal plant an oak tree if you need one that is particularly strong. Just take care of one. Help it grow and you will grow with it.

No one but someone who truly has lost his soul should say they do not have time for a plant. And this does not mean buying a potted plant and having your secretary take care of it or spending huge amounts of money on landscaping and letting gardeners do all the work. It means having a personal plant that relies on you to help it achieve greatness. The essence of personal responsibility and self-esteem can be found in this activity. It will be of great benefit to all, and no government program will be required, no counseling, no coalition of teachers or preachers or community leaders. I urge you to give it a try.

CHOOSING A LIFE PATH

Choosing your path in life is an ongoing process of decision-making. Contrary to what some might believe, our life path is not set out straight in front of us. The Angel of North America calls it a path, she says, because it is small and it is individual. No one ever has been down yours before. Your path, as is everyone's, is littered with obstructions. It is appropriate to call it a path because it can lead you to heaven. But you will have to weave your way along, watch your step, and be careful not to stray. The road to hell, on the other hand, is an eight lane super-highway. And there is no speed limit.

Does it matter what path you choose? No. There are endless possibilities, a myriad of twists and turns that a person may take during his lifetime. The more decisions you make in life, the quicker you will move ahead and the more possibilities that will open to you.

The more opportunities you have to make new decisions, the better. Why? Making decisions exercises your free will and the more you use your free will the better chance you have of becoming strong. Making right decisions helps your soul to fill. Making decisions helps you to become a better person. It helps you reach an understanding of the meaning of life. The stronger you are, the better able you will be to recognize evil when you see it and the better able you will be to fight it.

At the outset of our lives each of us has the goal of saving our soul. This is the meaning of life, as The Teacher reiterates over and over. Saving your soul is why you and others are here on earth. The earth went along fine without humans for hundreds of millions of years. Man's existence here is an opportunity to prove his worthiness and loyalty to God.

Some believe that their path in life is predetermined, but I am assured by The Teacher that this is not the case. Your path must be created anew every day through the force of your will. People must overcome the obstacles that are placed in front of them. Handicaps come in all sorts of shapes and sizes. They may be a physical handicap of some kind, an illness, the geography of your birth, or the economic standing of your parents. Not everyone has equal abilities. Not everyone has the same opportunities in life. But everyone does have two things in common. We all have free will. Every one of us has talents. Everyone has the ability to use those talents to achieve his goal.

A major problem in our society is that most of us have lost sight of the real goal of life in this physical realm of earth. We set goals for ourselves to be sure, but these goals usually revolve around such things as political power, wealth, fame, prestige in business, or the achievement of some feat or standing in a sport. These are worthwhile endeavors, but they may not help you advance toward the goal of saving your soul.

The meaning of life is to save your soul. Any goal other than this may distract you from the reason you are here. It may cloud your vision. It may be an obstruction. The goal may divert your attention so that you do not recognize the temptation evil places in your path. Evil is constantly working to capture your soul.

The Teacher tells us that we need not worry about

choosing the absolute best possible path, the absolute best thing to do. Some believe that each person has a specific mission in a given lifetime. While individuals do incarnate with specific missions from time to time, this is not true of every individual. Rather, each incarnation should be viewed as a potentiality. The mission of life is to live that potentiality to the fullest. Everyone's talents can be used in a variety of ways. Just because someone is smart and has a wonderful ability to learn and to solve problems does not mean they must become a scientist or a mathematician. Because someone has exceptional athletic ability does not mean they can only be a baseball or a football player. Nor should one feel he must do the same thing all through his life. Keeping the same job, staying in the same position, advancing through the ranks of a company does not assure success as a person. If you allow all your decisions to be made for you, if you go through life simply letting things happen and reacting to circumstances rather than seeking out and making decisions, you will not grow spiritually.

The Teacher says that no excuse exists for not maturing spiritually. If you do not recognize this fact, no one is to blame but yourself. You will be held accountable and may not receive another opportunity.

Children need to be taught this. In the past people have hidden the meaning of life as if it were some sort of secret, as if it were some sort of goal that had to be searched for. This is a waste. People should not spend their time searching for the meaning of life. Children should be told early what the meaning of life is. It is a concept that they may not understand. Nevertheless, there is no reason to hide it from them. The concept of saving one's soul is true and belongs in every religion, every culture, every household. All people have souls. They need to know what to do with them. It is unfair to ask children what they want to do and become in life without letting them know the most important thing of all they must do.

Our society as a whole has tended to ignore evil and to treat it as though it does not exist. Can we ignore cancer? Can we ignore a flood? Can we ignore sunshine in the morning? Evil is the same kind of force. It is there. It is real. It gets in our way. If God did not have a need for souls to prove themselves, if the need did not exist for every spirit to be given the opportunity to choose, there would be no reason for man to be on earth. There would be no reason for each of us to choose a path. If this need did not exist, everyone would live in peace and harmony and do the right things. There would be no conflict and no pain. Life would not exist as we know it and there would be no need to choose.

If you do not believe evil exists, take a careful look at today's newspaper. Pay attention to the evening news. It is right there in front of you.

We each need to make our way through life. We need to make our path so that our children can follow in our footsteps and continue when our time is over. About the age of fifteen or sixteen in our society children reach a level of maturity when they begin making their own decisions. A great many problems today stem from these young adults being in a position to make decisions without the benefit of complete knowledge. They need to have learned as children the difference between right and wrong and between good and evil. They need to have learned from having suffered the consequences of their decisions.

A popular misconception is that evil is not rewarded. This creates confusion in young people because evil rewards quickly. Children need to know this. No limit exists as to when evil can begin affecting a person. It starts at the beginning of a child's life when temptations are presented. It begins by the rewarding of decisions that were made with the wrong intent.

Let us consider an example. Some teenagers are

talking after school about getting together and having a good time. Someone brings beer. Everyone knows they should not drink it but because of peer pressure they all do. Because everyone joins in this group activity, it makes them all feel good. This is evil rewarding their negative behavior. The rewards of evil come immediately and often.

Evil reinforces wrong behavior. The rewards for good behavior, on the other hand, take longer to realize. Wrong behavior is difficult to change. This is how evil first affects the body, then drains the soul.

As these young people mature, much of their bad behavior becomes set in place. As they learn and grow in wisdom it will become increasingly difficult for them to change. Temptations will become harder to fight. Once they stop fighting, their soul is drained. By middle age, a great number will feel the emptiness. They will not have the zest and vitality they had when they were younger. This is the time on their path when they either lose their spiritual side altogether or realize they are losing it and begin an earnest fight to regain it. This is the point on the path where it is hardest to keep going.

Mid life is in fact the time when most realize they are indeed on a path. They understand that life is difficult. They are not sure when or how they got where they are or precisely where they are headed. For others mid life can be the time they realize they are on a super highway going a hundred miles an hour but that even this high speed is not fast enough to satisfy them.

What should a person do when he has taken his own path and is not sure where he is or where he is headed? Say, for example, you have been making decisions throughout your life. Your soul is intact. You may have had temptations but you certainly have not given over to evil. You question your career, your finances, what you have done with your life. Or perhaps you are in another group. You are on the highway and you are moving along but you are not very satisfied. There is not even any attractive scenery along the way. You do not have time to smell the flowers. All your life you have been going in the same direction, doing the same thing. You would like to get off and are looking for a place. You know this road is wrong for you but you are in the middle of sixteen lanes and cannot seem to get over to the side. You see exit signs but you cannot maneuver through the traffic. It keeps you hurling in a direction you no longer want to go.

In both cases, the answer is spirituality. You need to find a religion or a spiritual group of some kind. You need to find a structure that will allow you to be with other people so that you can experience the energy of God. This is the energy of goodness and of meaning. It is the energy that comes to a group when they pray.

Many people want to have direct contact with God. When God does not answer their personal requests they become disappointed and disillusioned. They may give up.

The Teacher tells us that God does not answer every question, every prayer, every request. But she also says he does not ignore you. There is a flow of energy that is the well of goodness on the earth. God does not have to answer your prayers for you to feel this. He does not have to answer your prayers for you to become part of the energy and to be renewed by it.

Once you recognize the energy, once you believe that it is real and are sincere in your belief, God will answer your prayers. But this does not come without faith. God will not come to you with a sign that says to change your ways or your beliefs. You must go to him. That is the whole idea behind free will. The devil comes to you. The devil wants you. God wants you, too, but God asks you to make the choice. Once you have been renewed, once you have had the experience of the energy of goodness, it will become easier to find the right path of your life. It will become easier to recognize temptations. You will still struggle with temptation but you begin to know where you are headed.

What about those who are headed down the highway of life, doing a hundred and twenty in their BMW and passing everyone they can? These people may not be sure where they are headed but they definitely want to get there first. If you are like this, you had better pray you have a flat tire or that there is an accident up ahead, something to slow you down, because as you bolt farther and farther ahead in the passing lane you will notice there are fewer and fewer drivers. No one else wants to be up there with you because you are on the road to hell.

You are not going to drive off the edge all of a sudden, or be engulfed in a fireball of flame and pain. You will just keep going the way you have been. There will be fewer and fewer cars around until you recognize you are on the road all alone. You have reached the point in your career when there is no where else to go. You are at the top. There is no one around you can talk to. There is no one else that understands what you have done or where you are.

You now have the choice of repenting, or not. You can give it all up and totally change your life, or you can be destroyed by the emptiness. The emptiness you feel will be a small taste of hell. Some people do come back. They have been at the top, and they have given it all up. These are the folks who tell the story of finding new meaning in life. They find it in their family. They find it in helping others. These are the survivors. Most of them, however, die alone. They die empty and damned. This sounds harsh, but they have gotten where they have ended up of their own free will.

We have discussed mid life. What about the end of life? Like it our not, this is a time that will come if you hang in there. This is when you are old enough to realize that you could die any day. It is a time of reflection. It is a time of contemplation and of self-searching. If you have led a good life and are secure in your faith, you will know that your soul is full. You will be ready and happy and accepting of death. If you have not led such a good life and are not secure in your faith, you will not be sure where you stand. You will be fearful. You may now question your denial of evil, your denial of heaven, your denial of the spiritual realm. You question and question and finally you repent before you die.

It may not be too late but it will not be easy. For many people the realization comes too late. Although they want to be in touch with the energy and want to believe in God, there may not be enough of their soul left to save them.

As long as there is any soul left, there is a chance for you to be with God. But, if you are so old that you could die any day, you have no path left. You do not have time to fill your soul on this trip to earth. You are too near the end.

You will face a decision. It is one you will not be able to hide from. You will not be able to ignore it and it will not be made for you. You will have to decide whether or not you want to try again or to await God's judgment. This will not be easy. No one but God knows when the judgment is coming, not even The Angel of North America.

So you pass over to the other side and find you are not in the energy. You soon realize you will not be with God and will have to wait for his decision concerning your fate. If you choose to try again, you will not know when your opportunity will come. When it does, you will have to start all over. You will have no memory, no advantage of the experience of your previous life. You will have to make decisions again. You will have to choose your path. You will have to fight evil. But at least you will have the opportunity to try once again.

How can you know if your life is good? Your conscience will tell you.

Perhaps you do not know if you have a conscience. If this is so, it is gone.

The Teacher tells us that leading a good life does not mean one always has to do everything right. Humans give in to temptation. They make mistakes. They do bad things. To be a good person one must fight evil, repent for mistakes and do good things for others. One needs to praise God and use the talents wisely that God gave him.

You will know you are doing good when you are happy. You will know when you have good relationships with others. You will know when others are not controlling you and you are not controlling others. There will be a lightness in your heart, a buoyancy in your solar plexus. You will recognize temptation. You will be able to feel the energy of goodness.

How can you know what this energy is? How can you feel it?

At first you will not notice it until it is gone. You will be with a group of people and they will make you feel good. You will not be sure what made you feel good but you will realize when you leave the group that something is missing. It will be a kind of longing. When this happens you have experienced the energy of goodness.

Next, you will feel the energy when you do good for others, when you go out of your way to do something for somebody else. I am not talking writing a big check to a charity. This is like asking someone else to do a good deed on your behalf. I am talking about when you go out and do it yourself. You will feel good. There will be a glow that comes over you. This is the energy of goodness filling your soul.

Here is an example. When floods hit in the Midwest a few years ago, people would drive for hundreds of miles to help fill sandbags and to attempt to save the homes of people they did not even know. These people felt good about what they were doing. When a person takes the time and volunteers for the Red Cross to handle donations, when they take the time to answer questions or to help people who have lost their homes, they often inexplicably will feel a tingle inside. People they do not know will come up and thank them for what they are doing. Energy comes to them and fills their soul. They know in this way that they are on the right life path.

One cannot have too much goodness in their soul. The soul does not fill up with goodness and begin to spill out. The soul is not a fixed vessel that can only hold so much. It keeps on filling. One does not have to be rich. One does not have to gain possessions. One does not have to be attractive or to do great things to feel this energy. One simply has to get on and stay on the right path.

The Teacher urges you, and I urge you, to begin your personal journey on the path of goodness. Join with the flow by planting a seed or caring for a plant. Nurture it and help it grow. You will share the energy with this plant. It will be a reflection of the goodness growing within you. If you care for this plant and have a good life, it too will grow and be healthy and strong. If you see the plant begin to wither or fade, it will be a prompt to examine your life. Look for temptations. Think about the decisions you have made or have not made. Examine your life by evaluating who is in control. If there are problems, fix them. Do more for others. Be responsible for your own actions. Change what you are doing so that others do not control you. Regain control and fight evil whenever you encounter it. Get a new plant once you have made the necessary changes to your life so that it will be a proper reflection of how you have changed. This is the advice I bring to you from The Angel of North America, a messenger of God.

CHOOSING A MATE

Now let us consider the matter of choosing a mate, a life partner which whom you can chart and find your path. Maturity should be the starting point. There first needs to be a sense of readiness, knowledge and security in one's abilities to cope with the problems of the world. A spouse should not be a crutch. A spouse should be a partner. Each should be able to stand alone before the couple is joined. God expects people to be together, to grow together and after a period to have their spirits so unified that they are able to think of themselves as one. This is the ideal. In the world there are many problems to be dealt with. The Teacher has given a few basic insights which if heeded can help eliminate problems in choosing a path and the correct person for a mate.

First, age makes a difference. Choose someone who is close to your own. Find someone with similar interests, similar background, the same religion, the same race. This advice, especially the latter, is sure to raise the eyebrows of some. But it makes basic common sense. Life will run more smoothly if you share it with someone who has similar interests, views and upbringing. Life will be more pleasant if there is commonality in the things you do and enjoy. This will help keep the two of you together because you will both enjoy participating in the similar activities. One of the key reasons for getting married is to have fun with someone. So pick someone you will enjoy being with, someone who can help make your life exciting and special.

Finding someone with similar interests will help you avoid conflict. If you are a woman and the two things you like to do most are to go shopping and dancing and you have decided to marry a lawyer who hates shopping and dancing and wants to spend all his free time in a bar, you are headed for problems. You are not going to see this fellow much. You are going to resent the fact that he does not spend time with you. He is going to resent your spending his money. You probably will not like his friends. What you have is a disaster waiting to happen.

Finding someone with common interests helps eliminate the need for one partner to control the other. Evil works its ways easily in bad marriages. The worst situation is the one in which a person marries strictly for love and is blind to other aspects of the object of her love. The physical attraction one feels in the first contact with someone, or the lack of it, is important in helping to eliminate suitors, but it is not a good basis a long-term relationship. Certainly not marriage.

Few people have the opportunity to get to know the spiritual side of their prospective mate before they marry. So, it is necessary that you do whatever you can to find as much commonality in your personalities and in your goals and beliefs as you possibly can before making a commitment.

You will be better off choosing someone with a similar background for many of the same reasons. Having a feeling for how someone grew up, for the size of their family, for where they lived, who their parents, grandparents and ancestors were, also helps eliminate conflict later in a marriage. For example, say you are a young, wealthy man who came from a family that has been wealthy for several generations. You possess the expectations that come along with this heritage. Your family has expectations for you. Upon entering the job market you fall in love with your secretary. She has no money. She comes from a large family and is very close to them. She is beautiful and funny. You are physically attracted to her and you like to be with her. You decide to get married.

Here is what you can look forward to. She will not want to leave her family and move around the country. She will call and talk to her mother three times a day. She will want to spend every other weekend visiting them. She will not be comfortable spending money. Your parents will be cold and distant toward her. This is another disaster waiting to happen. This marriage will not last.

As was discussed earlier, when you marry you should do so with the expectation that it is for life. There are circumstances when this is not possible. There are circumstances when it is not healthy, when it is not good for either individual. But the expectation at the outset should be that this will be your life partner until one of you dies. You should have the expectation of having children, of growing old together, of meeting each other's needs, of helping each other find spiritual fulfillment. The expectation should be that when you die you will both go to heaven. It is difficult enough to live with another person and to have a union without one partner having to make up for the other's faults or shortcomings. Entering into a marriage with someone who has a great deal of excess baggage because of inherent differences which should have been identified is asking for trouble.

The relationship of marriage affects the path you choose in life in uncountable ways. First, choosing someone with a similar background will mean that you will not have to go through a lot of explanations about why one person handles their problems a certain way or has a particular outlook on life or about what their goals will be in a given situation. There will be many points in a relationship when you will be on a circular path. Without similar backgrounds you will constantly be trying to go off in different directions. You will be pulling against each other instead of working your way through a problem and moving on. Without a similar background the partners will be spending time throughout their marriage, from the first year to the fiftieth, constantly making each other aware of their intentions. In some ways this may seem interesting. Nevertheless, it will be more difficult than necessary for each partner to achieve their goals.

The greatest happiness will come if a couple can realize a spiritual joining early in their marriage. The different stages of love can then grow and evolve beyond that spiritual bonding. If it takes fifteen years for a couple to reach the point of spiritual bonding, half of their married life may be gone before they move on to higher levels of love and understanding of one another. If it cannot be reached within the first three to five years of marriage, the couple is doing something wrong. They each have picked the wrong mate. Something in the relationship is getting in the way and the obstacle needs to be removed before love can mature.

People make mistakes in choosing their mates. It is a human condition. It is very difficult in our society to make the right choice. There is pressure to marry young. There is pressure to have sex. There is pressure to achieve material wealth and its trappings. There is an underlying liberal philosophy that it is all right to do anything one likes. This is wrong. Choosing a mate is serious business. It should be done one time and one time only. It needs to be done right the first time. Making mistakes in choosing a mate opens a person to the control of evil. Having the wrong mate bleeds energy. It weakens a person both mentally and spiritually. It is a situation that is very difficult to recover from.

If you make a mistake in choosing because your partner has been dishonest, or if they try to manipulate you or to keep things hidden, talk to a priest or seek help from some other spiritual counselor as soon as you find out. You need to take action at the first signs of evil coming into your marriage or the outcome can be detrimental for both you and your partner. Even though you may love your mate, the force of evil working through them can take your soul. As The Teacher has said many times, **the meaning of life is to save your soul.** Your life partner should be there to nurture your spiritual energy, not to drain it away.

Let us finish this discussion with the touchy subject of race. If you marry outside of your race it does not mean that you are damned to hell. But, as in previous examples, your life will be more difficult than it needs to be. Making your life harder is not what being married should be all about. There is an old saying that if you want to make your life difficult walk through life with a goat tied to you. This is what it is like to be married outside of your race. It is just plain difficult. The Teacher assures us that God will give us enough to overcome in a marriage to make it challenging. It is not necessary to go outside one's race to make it doubly so.

JUDGMENT

Let us turn our attention to the subject of judgment. There are many sides to this issue. A person is constantly being judged by her family, her friends, others in the community, her boss, her children. People are judged according to what they do and how they act towards others. The only judgment one does not have to worry about is God's. We are told by The Teacher that God is open, forgiving and full of true love. God does not judge an individual on a day-to-day basis. She says the truth is, you really do not have to worry about God's judgment until the final judgment comes, and then only if you happen to be here on earth and your life is not over. Otherwise, you do not have to worry about judgment at all.

Here on earth we have to deal with other humans and with temptations and our bodies and our needs. We judge each other in order to form concepts of how to function in society. This is necessary. Without some basis of judgment of good and bad and right and wrong, we would be lost. We have become a society of people not knowing what to do. By not passing judgment on the actions and deeds of others, we placidly accept their behavior. As a result, people do not know when they are doing something wrong because everything is acceptable. There is no judgment.

The judgments of peers, or "peer pressure" as it is called, forms the basis of the actions of the society. If there is no peer pressure to be good, people will not be good. If there is no peer pressure to obey traffic signs, no one will obey them. Peer pressure works.

Unfortunately, in our society a positive, focused, society-wide standard of what is right and what is wrong is missing. It has been lost because of the liberal attitude that we should not judge one another. The Teacher tells us that this is one aspect of our society that we must change. If we do not judge each other, if we do not straighten out our uncaring attitudes toward each other, God will do it for us.

There is a popular misconception that following our physical death there will be some sort of judgment of whether or not we are going to get into heaven. We are told by the angels that this is not the whole truth. The truth is that to a great extent we choose whether or not we will go to heaven while we are here on earth. If you have not gotten this message already, **the meaning of life is to save your soul.** The purpose of saving your soul is to go to heaven. If you do not save your soul, you will not go to heaven. There is nothing magical that happens after the last breath of your life, the time your soul is released, that will change how you have lived and how you have chosen to exercise your free will. If you have allowed your soul to be emptied and drained, it will be empty and drained. If you choose to ignore God while here on earth, what is going to make you find God once you are dead? If you choose to not join with the energy of the universe through prayer and to touch others in a spiritual way, what makes you think that you will have the opportunity to do so once you are dead?

When you are dead you will have no more choices. You will have no more free will. You will either wait for the

97

judgment at the end of the world when God will make a decision on those souls who have not prepared, or you have to try again if you are even given the opportunity. Some believe that if they repent just before they die everything will be all right. They will have salvation. The Teacher says that anyone who believes this is fooling himself. Yes, there is a loving, merciful God, but he is also a God who has given man free will. God does not interfere with a man's life, but the devil does. The devil will try to entice you. He will reward you. The devil can make life very, very pleasant. The devil will also take your soul. You can give up your soul to the devil. People do it all the time and they do not even realize that they have made a choice. Once you have given your soul to the devil it is too late to say at your last moment of life, "Oops, I made a mistake." The choice already has been made and you made it. There will be sorrow and regret in heaven about this. Nevertheless, God lets us choose. By the time you reach your death bed your choice already will have been made.

How good does one have to be in order to go to heaven?

The Teacher says it not a matter of how good one is but of how full her soul is. The energy that fills your soul is fluid. Points are not given for doing good deeds. Points are not given for praying. No points are scored for praising God. But when you do these things, energy flows into you and you grow in strength and you grow in knowledge and you become confident in wisdom to make the right decisions.

There is a constant, daily struggle against temptation. Any day you can give in to it. Any day you can disobey the Commandments. Any day you can let yourself become drained through greed or envy. Any day you can give over some of the control, some of the decisions in your life to evil. When you do, you will be drained.

The stronger you are, the fuller your soul is, the harder

it is for evil to drain your soul. A strong person is not likely to wake up one morning and sell his soul for a lottery ticket. So it is not how good you are but how strong a person you are in the spiritual sense. You can become strong and fill your soul throughout your life. This is what wins a place in heaven.

Each person is his own judge. You judge yourself by the decisions you make and the way you live your life. You judge yourself by whether you choose to accept or reject God. People always ask, "What if I don't believe in heaven? What if I don't believe in God? What will happen to me then?"

You have made a choice and will get what you choose. The part of you that is spirit, your soul, will be without God. You will be alone. You will be empty. You will be in hell.

People ask, "What if I lived a good life, but then strayed?"

Come back. Repent. Repent. Repent. As was said earlier, this is not a competition where points are scored. If you led a good life early on and then fell victim to temptation, you are being drained. The energy is flowing out of you. If you are not constantly filling your soul with energy you are not doing what is necessary to keep yourself a whole person. You must be whole both physically and spiritually.

Let me give you an example. A young man goes through college and enters the business world as a banker. I will call him Adam. For twenty years Adam does an outstanding job making his business grow, helping the community, being an exemplary leader for his employees. One day a politician comes by and asks Adam to handle his account. Large amounts of cash begin flowing in. Every so often there are separate envelopes that come to Adam which are for his personal use. Because Adam has been a strong person he is in touch with the energy. He knows that something is wrong, but he decides not to investigate. Adam pockets the money and keeps his mouth shut. At first his conscience bothers him terribly. But the more money he receives the less desire he has to find out where it is coming from.

At the end of a year, an auditor comes in and discovers that the politician is running a money laundering scheme. Adam, his reputation now on the line, becomes depressed. The pressure from the media is just too much to bear. One night after dinner he has a heart attack and dies.

Now what will happen to Adam? Even though he spent twenty years living a good life, the past year has drained him nearly dry. He chose not to do what his conscience told him. He chose not to bring his suspicions to the attention of the authorities. He chose to become a tool of the evil force. In essence, Adam rejected God.

After his death, Adam will have to choose either to await God's judgment at the end of the world or to await an opportunity to try again. Reincarnation will not be automatic. During Adam's stay in limbo while he waits, he will be without God's love, without his energy. Adam will exist in constant fear of the rejection that could take place on the final Day of Judgment.

A major goal of this book is to let everyone know who will listen that awaiting judgment is not a position we must place ourselves in. We can each live full and happy lives. We can live them with the understanding that we can go to heaven. Everyone has the choice, the opportunity and the ability to go to heaven on his own. Positive thinking is not enough. We must know what to do. We must understand the difference between right and wrong. We must tell others the difference and make it absolutely clear so that they too can save their souls.

God knows all. God sees all. There is no hiding our intent when we accept evil. God cannot be fooled. If you accept evil into your life, be prepared for the outcome. You may fool yourself, but you will never fool God. And do not be fooled by the word, "intent." You can never "mean" to do the right thing but accidentally do the wrong thing. You cannot "mean" to do a good deed and then hurt someone. You cannot "mean" to go into a bank to make a deposit and then rob it. You cannot "mean" to love someone and then have a baby outside of marriage you cannot care for. You cannot "mean" to teach your children a lesson and then abuse them. Good is good. Evil is evil. There is a sharp and distinct line that one crosses to do one or the other. Being human is to plot a course on one side or the other of that line. The wise individual constantly will make the corrections necessary to stay on the side of good. Temptation is a strong wind that would blow you off course. Your salvation depends on how good a navigator you can become in your lifetime.

No one knows how long the race is or how far he will need to go. It makes sense, then, to stay on the side of good. This is the wisdom and the knowledge imparted to me by God's messenger, The Angel of North America.

CHILDREN HAVING CHILDREN

The Teacher would like me to pass along some of her views on teenagers having children. First, she says, there should be fewer of them. Teenagers absolutely should not be parents. This simply does not work well and should be thoroughly discouraged. And, in her view, single teen mothers are criminals, pure and simple. That's right, criminals. They rob working people through the welfare allotments they receive. They clog schools with underdeveloped children. They burden us all because they simply do not have the resources to raise a child properly. Often their offspring become criminals which further burdens society.

Love is not enough in this society. We have gone beyond tribal ways and there is no turning back. The nature of human beings is to want more; never to be satisfied. Our nature is to reach for the stars. It is not right for children to make decisions that so strongly impact all facets of our society. There should be severe repercussions when they do so. The Teacher says that at an early age, say thirteen years, everyone should be given the facts of life. They need to know how babies are made and what is involved in taking care of a child. They need to know that once they have one their life will come to a screeching halt.

The Teacher says that if a teen does not have the resources to care for a new baby her parents should become responsible. Otherwise, the baby should be put up for adoption. The father of that baby also should be affected for a long, long time. She is adamant about this. Estimates should be made periodically concerning the cost of raising a child and the father should have to pay. For example, in 1994 it cost $9,700 for the care of a newborn for the first year of its life. Since a fifteen year old boy can be expected to earn nothing at this stage of his life he will have just opened up a debit account. The next year the baby will cost him a $5,300 debit. By the time this young man reaches drinking age, the baby will have cost him $30,000. He will have to pay this or suffer all the consequences a society can bring to bear. He will not be able to get a driver's license, potential employers will be notified, the IRS will attach his wages, his life will be scrutinized by social workers, he will be denied a marriage license. If at this time he should be uncooperative with authorities, forgiveness of the debt can be made by submitting to a permanent vasectomy.

The Teacher says that she can promise that within five years the teen pregnancy problem will be nil if we enact her advice. Of course a lot of "rights" that irresponsible people now have will have been replaced by obligations. But the net result will be a better society, righting the balance of good and evil in the world and we will have been saved from God's impending punishment.

Some no doubt will ask, "Isn't this a bit extreme?"

Is it any more extreme than subjecting a new life to poverty, despair, abuse, and the lost opportunity to be part of a loving family? We need to get our priorities straight. We cannot walk away from this problem any longer. The liberal attitude must go. Our society is at the the brink of disaster and we brought ourselves to it. The overwhelming crime problem is but one of the warning signs. Professionals in social services have been telling us for thirty years what problems teen pregnancy causes. Yet our leaders refuse to address the heart of the issue and now the situation is out of hand. Teens who get pregnant, and those who sit by and allow them to do so, are hurting everyone. The time has come to get tough.

What has been outlined above, for human beings to be accountable for their actions, is no more than what responsible parents face when they bring home a precious newborn baby. Why should some who have not prepared properly be freed of responsibilities? Because they are young? Because they made a mistake? It is true. They have made a mistake, and it is time that they paid for it. A new life should not be taken so lightly. This comes directly from The Angel of North America, a messenger of God.

EDUCATION

People are taking more of an interest in their children's education today than they have in the past 25 years. A larger variety of materials to work with than ever before is available and in many cases children are more sophisticated and ready to learn then ever. Unfortunately, federal mandates take away parents' control of their children's educations more than ever. The cost of education per pupil has never been higher. Standardized testing is coming under attack from every quarter. Many groups would like to see IQ scores abandoned. The public demands accountability but does not wish to test pupils' knowledge. College is becoming more expensive because of huge increases necessary in remedial classes. By and large businesses feel that students are not prepared for work. Busing is still a nightmare. Up to 30% of a student's day is taken with social education. Classes are getting larger. Children are game-literate, but computing skills often are low or non-existent. It is ever more difficult to hold students' attention. Schools are constantly asked to do more, and everyone is tired.

The bad news outweighs the good. We cannot build on the good news until we take care of the problems. As a middle manager in education, I have seen first hand that the problems go both ways. School administrators are constantly asking for help, advice and direction. There is no lack of this from the private sector. People always are eager to say that schools should be run like businesses. The problem is that schools are not businesses. There is also plenty of advice coming from the federal government, which is loaded with lawyers and bureaucrats who have their own agendas but do not know education. Parents have needs, ideas and suggestions that they want to have incorporated into their children's schools. Teachers have ideas and lessons in education from a variety of professionals and outside sources. Local school boards of elected citizens feel that they have to be watchdogs of the publics' funds. Then there are the hired professionals, the education administrators. There are always "too many" of them doing jobs that are considered useless but that need to get done. Administration is a very large budget item in every community and state in the country.

Where do we start correcting these wrongs? Every local school superintendent has to deal with fixed budget items, keep up student test scores, provide breakfast, lunches, disabled services, transportation to and from home, counseling services, record keeping, payroll, health services, AIDS education, sex education, diversity education, drug education, and be available to answer any parent's question immediately as well as those of the media and the government. The list goes on and on.

School boards face the problem of having to pay for education by taxing everyone when only about 30% of the population have children in school. They have to be concerned with what is being taught in the schools. This is deemed much too demanding a job to expect professional educators to understand and deal with, so additional layers of bureaucracy are established. On the state and federal levels bureaucrats need to establish rules and keep records to set the standards for what should be done in the schools. Everyone has a say except the people being educated and those who need to have educated young adults coming into the workplace.

During the last 20 years management techniques in education generally have changed every two to four years. This is a problem. New ways of thinking cannot easily be plugged in to a program that needs to run for 12 years. As a result, children constantly miss things. Their education in academics is being cut short and the curriculum is being overloaded with liberal social skills. Some have the same academic classes repeated three times during their 12 year program and miss whole sections that were taught 40 or 50 years ago. There is a saying that times change. Nevertheless, some things need to remain the same. Proper grammar, word study, reading, writing, history, science, mathematics and citizenship are the corner stones of education. These basics have not changed in 200 years. Yet we try to change them. As a result, our children lack basic skills. Education is not a business nor is it a bureaucracy. Education is a form of communication. It is the passing on of information from one generation to the next. It should not be run for profit or influence. Rather, it should be a hallmark for all that is good in a society.

Education can be the engine that pulls a society forward to become a civilization. The workers, teachers and administrators in an educational system can lay a solid foundation, or they can make bricks of clay that wash away and leave nothing for future generations to build upon. The end result of education should be for a society to have common goals and standards that all can relate to and live by. We lack these common goals and uniform standards because of liberal attitudes.

Liberalism is a way of thinking, not a political affiliation. Liberal thinking, as The Teacher defines it, is leaving one's mind open to every point of view. It is the accepting of every standard and of everyone's way of doing things.

Liberalism is a state of mind that says that whatever one does is okay with me because I am open-minded. I accept your ways. In 1996, this is what the word liberal means in our society. The Teacher tells us without qualification that this is wrong. It is wrong for the society. It is wrong for management. It is wrong for education.

Liberalism has no place in an institution such as education. This does not mean that change cannot take place. This does not mean that education need be static and rigid. Nevertheless, education must have a focus.

It should be the task of schools to give children the tools, both physical and intellectual, that they need in order to acquire the knowledge and skills necessary to become productive members of the society. Children are a part of a society but should not become franchised until they go to work. Work is important to the human spirit. It is part of the natural order. Going against human nature by not sufficiently preparing our children to take their proper place in the natural order is detrimental to the good of the society.

Children cannot be prepared if school systems constantly inflict social experiments on them. Schools should be such that every generation knows exactly what is going on with their children in a given grade level. Everyone in an entire society should be taught the same math, the same language, the same history and social aspects of the culture. This is what will make education worthwhile.

There should be no "better" schools or "worse" schools. There should be none of the constant arguments and knee jerk reactions, reactions that cause turmoil and loss of continuity in a program. This is why there is no place for liberals in education. Constantly trying new things in the classrooms does not help children. It may be nice to give the teachers a break or for administrators to make a name for themselves or for them to become politicians, but it does no good for the children. Children do not know what is different. They do not care what is different. Children will learn what is taught them. Young people have only one opportunity to learn what they need to know. Then they go on. If a teacher gets tired of teaching the same thing over and over for years, the teacher should be changed, not what they teach. Children are no different now that they were thousands of years ago. They were easily distracted then and are easily distracted now. They were eager to play then, just as they are now. They picked on each other then, as now; were subject to the same peer pressures in ancient Greece or Rome as they are today in Indiana or California.

Children have an expectation that they are being prepared to take the place of their parents. Their parents know what the children need in order to take their places. In our society the parents should have input by elected officials to set the standards for what the children need in a particular geographical area. If they live in a place where primary employment is in the farming sector, most of the children will accept being prepared for those jobs. This is what they know and how they live. Farming for a living becomes their expectation. It is the view of liberal thinkers, however, that the children of those employed in agriculture should be required to broaden their horizons. It is their view that these children need to study something different. Why? There is no good reason. Moreover, this is against human nature.

People who live in cities and work in offices and factories will imprint the idea on their children of working in offices or factories. Educational goals should be set accordingly. There is no reason why everyone must move away from home, that everyone has to go far away to find fulfilling work. Such an idea is wrong headed. This is what tears family units apart.

The Teacher tells us that the idea that the family unit

is not important has its basis in our educational system. How many parents say they want to have the best for their children? Their view of the best is something that they have not achieved. This view creates unrealistic expectations that are nurtured by the schools and the education system. Everyone is encouraged to seek their own personal fulfillment instead of finding a place in society that is good for the society as well as the individual. This expectation tears family units apart. Children grow up feeling that their parents do not have the best life, that the best life is somewhere else where they will be doing something different than what their parents did. The result is that no one ever can be satisfied. No one ever can be happy.

This needs to be changed if society is to advance. It is human nature that people appreciate their families. It is human nature that they stay with their families and that family units grow and prosper in proximity to one another. Our society has made a huge and expensive business out of trying to bring families back together by telephone. Telephones have allowed people to live farther and farther apart and still try to remain connected. An incredibly strong attraction exists for families to remain together and connected. People who own communication systems know and exploit this aspect of human nature. They are constantly working and striving to bring families back together. Images in TV commercials show people who are happy and joyful talking to one another on telephones. These people feel a sense of belonging because they can call home and be with their loved ones. These people are fighting human nature by being apart. Human nature is for people to stay together in family units.

Eventually family units grow to the point where some members indeed leave. Traditionally, these were females who became members of another strong and tightly knit male-dominated family core. Single mothers, female heads of households, have no way to maintain that ancient and mysterious bond. The more liberal attitudes are accepting of this way of life, the more that families will be torn apart. As people accept single-mother households as a normal way of life, the society will be torn apart. Not because of uncaring, terrible people, but because this way goes against basic human nature. Human nature will not change no matter how sophisticated the society becomes or how advanced the thinking is. No matter how liberal the society may feel it has become, basic human nature will prevail. Human nature is an incredibly strong force and if the society does not conform to it, society will fail. Society then will begin again along the lines that are consistent with human nature. This is a major reason why education is failing our young people.

The liberal view of education is to prepare young people for life. The Teacher's view of education is to prepare people to work to be productive members of society. Only experience can prepare people for life. The educational institution cannot do it all. Bureaucrats in Washington have continued piling on mandates and programs to the extent that education has become a farce. So where do we go?

Before this century, most education was done in very small groups. People received a basic education but the vast majority gained their education through apprenticeship. They learned how to read and write, to communicate, and to have rudimentary skills in mathematics. But the real education came through an apprenticeship. Mill workers had to become skilled mathematicians. It was one thing to read blueprints, but it is another to work out the tolerances and to know the idiosyncrasies of complicated milling machines to be able to turn pieces of metal into usable parts. People did not go to school or to universities to become writers. They went to little papers, got jobs and practiced writing usually under an experienced editor. Nearly every facet of life had an apprentice program by which people learned their jobs and what to do in them. This is the basis for the simpler time that people long for.

In order for education to serve the public and to advance the goals of the society, it needs to be kept simple. Education today is not simple. Education is expected to do everything and to be everything to young people to make them full and well rounded adults. Without experience this cannot happen. Our educational system needs to get back to basics. Children need to be taught reading, writing and arithmetic. They need to study science literature and history. When they are old enough, they should have the option of learning a trade. Children should learn about life from life. They should learn what they need to know to make a living from school.

It should not be the government's job to tell people where they can go and what they can do with their lives. Yet, by taking the liberal view that the government should be in charge of education, this is exactly what is happening. This needs to be changed, and it is up to us as voters and taxpayers to insure that we elect officials who will make these changes.

GOVERNMENT

Government's role in this society has become too intrusive. Our constitution and the way our government acts today are in contradiction. On one hand, the schools teach children that America is the land of the free. On the other, many lawyers, civil rights groups and officials in the government are so intent on establishing people's rights, that people have so many rights freedom is taken away from them.

The concept of lawyers being a part of a society is good. But lawyers have become a burden by choking freedoms and closing off avenues of choice. In this way many have become tools of evil. This is particularly difficult for young people to understand. For example, the government now makes it mandatory that children be given social security numbers so that there will be a way to measure the government's success with its program of welfare. This is an intrusion. Moreover, the government should not view increased numbers receiving welfare as a success. It is a measure of the government's failure. Government should take care of only those children that are orphaned by war or natural disaster.

Over the years the government has sought new programs to help people. This is wrong. It is a family's job to help their own. But for government to grow and to survive it has tried to replace the family. This is an evil concept. The government cannot supply love and understanding and energy to people.

Something that The Teacher says stretches the limits of her ability to comprehend is our constant harping on the need for self-esteem. Somehow, it seems, the government is supposed to help people find it. She says that no amount of psychobabble can provide someone with self-esteem. The truth, she says, is that self-esteem comes from goodness. It comes from the positive energy that arises from an understanding of and a sharing in God's love. Without this, there is no self-esteem. No amount of mental or physical exercise or listening to self-help tapes will make a difference. No government program, no group dynamics or weekend retreats will give a person self-esteem. No amount of money, fame, or high level of achievement can give self-esteem. It cannot be learned. It cannot be bought. It cannot be sold. It can come only from God's love. And the government is the least likely vehicle to bring this positive energy of God to the people.

Why do we distrust the government? Because the government is in competition with the family. People inherently know that being part of a family is good. People feel dissatisfied on a subconscious level in a way that is difficult for them to express. They do not wish to accept that the government is hurting them. A good deal of talk has been bandied about lately of the need for less government and for change. The problem is, people do not know where to begin. This is true even of good-intentioned people who have recently joined the government with the intention of helping to stop the downward slide. The competition between government and family will not be eliminated until the concept of evil is accepted. Evil must be combated wherever it is attempting to hurt people. This is not the final word on the subject, but the place to begin is to reduce the number of laws in our society. Laws take away people's ability to make decisions.

Here is an example. The government sets up a tax system where people are supposed to pay a portion of their income in taxes. This act, in and of itself, is neither good nor bad. Taxes are necessary to promote the general welfare and to support the common goals of the people. Then another tax law is enacted that says that for some reason certain people do not have to pay a certain portion of the tax. If you can find a way not to pay the tax, then that is okay, that is your right as a citizen.

Then a whole list of rules and laws are enacted citing circumstances under which a citizen does not have to pay the tax. Whether a law is broken now becomes a matter of interpretation. This creates a situation that must be carefully policed. As a result, a system of checks and balances is established to monitor and control people, to catch those that cheat and to put the rest on notice that they had better not do anything wrong or the police will catch them. What is at fault here is a system that encourages people to try to cheat or at the very minimum to find loopholes.

It is not considered cheating if one can find a way to avoid a tax, no matter how convoluted, that falls within the law. Even so, a situation has been created where animosity may be felt toward those who avoid the tax by those who have to pay it. This system allows evil to gain control over people. With so many rules that are open for interpretation, a situation has been put in place where people must make an abundance of choices between good and bad. This is asking for trouble. People have temptation confronting them that did not have to be placed in their path. They can no longer simply give a fair and just amount of money to the government for taxes. There must be a prescribed way that they give the money. If these laws are not followed specifically, people are judged by the government to be bad. Laws are enacted to have them punished.

Evil feeds on this kind of logic and these kinds of man-made rules enacted to control people's lives. This is how the government becomes a tool of evil. The more rules that men make, the further they get from living by the Commandments. The more difficult it is to make their own decisions and moral justifications, the more difficult it is to be good and to keep their soul full of God's energy.

Many who are part of the government believe that the government is good. They believe that it is the government's function to have a law to cover every possible human circumstance. This is a function of the need lawyers feel to control others. Evil is the source of this. Government's true role is to protect the society and to keep it functioning as a cohesive unit. When the government takes away the opportunity and ability for people to make decisions and use free will, the government interferes with the purpose God has for man being on earth, which is for man to exercise free will in order to save his soul. The more that process of decision-making is hampered, the harder it is for people to become strong and to grow in energy and goodness and to achieve true self-esteem. This is why government's intervention into people's lives is detrimental to the society.

EVIL IN HIGH OFFICE

One day, in January, 1996, The Teacher came to me almost in a tirade, saying that she needed to speak out about the leader of our government. It is best, I feel, to quote her verbatim so that you will sense the emotion behind her words. I have set down here exactly what she said with only minor editing for clarification:

I need to speak out about this today to address an important example of the problems of your society. We have been reading news accounts of situations in the government dealing with the president and his problems with Congress, the attempts of congressional members to deal with an honest, balanced budget. I am in no way politically oriented, but I am very concerned with the aspects of character among the leadership. Your president is lying again about his views. He is misrepresenting facts and he is deceiving under the guise of political action. This is wrong. The man is not honest. The man is not truthful. His greed and ambition are overwhelmingly obvious in his actions. Herein lies a problem with Evil in your society. A good number of people know and recognize the leader's lies, yet they excuse it because he is a politician. Because he was trained as a lawyer it is difficult to know whether

117

he feels that it is his job to lie and deceive or that it is a part of his personality. Either way it is wrong. Now, it has happened in the past that when people recognized the lies and deceptions in their leaders they wouldn't stand for it. There was outrage and the leaders were forced to step aside. But now there is a tolerance. This is a vivid example of Evil in your society. This is the example of a liberal view by which people accept the lies and deceptions as part of their lives. It would be bad enough if this person were just a businessman, perhaps one who lied and deceived his customers in his retail business. When people realized his deceptive practices, it would be up to them to choose to deal with him or not. But this person is the leader of your society. He is someone who should be held up in high esteem. What he does affects nearly everyone in the society. And people accept it. It can't be helped but that many will model behavior after this leader and this type of behavior is wrong. Not part of the way wrong, not excusable wrong, not "Well other people are mean to him so this is what he has to do" wrong. This is just plain vanilla wrong. It should not be accepted and should not be tolerated. It is having Evil in your midst. This is the type of situation wherein if the devil were running for president he would win in a landslide. People are so accepting of these lies and deceptions that they are blind to them. They just accept them regardless of their political affiliation. This type of behavior should not be tolerated. When you let the evil into your society it drains everyone. It is one thing to have to deal with individuals in your life lying to you and to decide whether or not you are going to deal with them. The problem with people that lie is that they take energy from those who are good. The personal energy is drained and the community is weakened because certain members no longer can be trusted. It tends to bring on suspicion, mistrust, and a reluctance to deal and communicate with others. It weakens the fabric of the community. When your leader lies, it touches everyone's life and it will do so for years and years to come because of the policies they enact.

There is no question, there is no argument that the situation in your government is a grossly imbalanced budget. No one can deal with this for long in their daily lives. But the government is different. It has a separate life. It has a life and being beyond the collective spirit of all the members, and it affects all of the members in varying degrees. No one can escape taxes. No one can escape the laws. It is important to the society that the laws that you pass be fair and truthful and just for the health and well-being of the society. What sense does it make to try to fool and deceive people about balancing the budget? It is either balanced or it is not. If it is not, you have to borrow money, you have to use your credit and herein lies a great source of the Evil. Credit is advanced whether in heaven or on earth because of a person's integrity. When people pray and ask God for help, when they promise never to do bad things again, there is a pact made that implies truthfulness and honesty. In listening to your prayers there is an expectation that the behavior that is promised will be changed for the better. There has to be a level of truthfulness. Honesty is the base for which the credit is extended and the prayers are answered. When people lie about their intentions, when they lie year after year after year about balancing the budget, a lack of faith in the leader's word is certain to follow.

The society no longer trusts its leadership. It doesn't trust the laws. It doesn't trust the government. Other communities, other countries, different societies that you will have to deal with will not trust you when the punishment comes. There will be no faith in the government and it will collapse like a house of cards. The government will not be able to control the civil unrest because there is no integrity. People will say that you have lied and lied to us in the past, why should we believe you now? This is the natural order of things. God knows. God made this order. He set this natural order in place and this is why the punishment will destroy you. It is what you have done to yourself. It is the level of suspicion that you have for your leaders. You have grown to accept people that lie and deceive. This is why your society will be torn apart. It will be because there will be no trust. This is not a difficult concept to comprehend but it is the liberal view to accept such behavior as normal and to be held up in esteem. I can't tell you any more plainly that this is wrong. I cannot tell you who to choose for a leader. I can't make any recommendations. It is up to you to choose. But it is time for people to get upset about what is being done to them. It is time to get upset and take control back of your lives. Change the laws. Change the leadership. You have to change the fact that good people are doing nothing. This is very serious. This is one of the most serious situations.

Everyone talks about how bad crime is, how bad welfare is to the fabric of the society, but to maintain a leader who practices lies and deception, it borders on sin. If people make such bad choices they will be punished for them. This controls too many people's lives. This brings the power of Evil too close to absolute power to have nothing done about it.

Now, in some ways some people will think that it is not fair to put this much weight and responsibility on one person, but these are the times in which you live. If that person is too weak to stand up to the truth, he shouldn't be there. It is the liberal view to have acceptance and forgiveness. If I haven't said it before let me put it forth in another way. What is at stake here are peoples' souls.

When the punishment comes, it will be the final judgment for many—for all of those who participated in the lies and deception, for all of those who have accepted Evil into their lives. All their souls will be lost. Regardless of their intentions, regardless of what they may think they are doing to help, regardless of how they think that they will do better in the future, they will have to face judgment. If there has not been honesty, if there has not been an intent and positive actions toward following the Commandments and helping others, they will have made their own judgment of themselves. Their fate will have been set and they will have to face God with the life that they have lived. Everyone who dies will be in this position.

People have a liberal view of a merciful and accepting God. But God did create hell for those who are not worthy, and for those who choose not to be with him. This liberal view of a merciful God is wishful thinking. Everyone should have the information that they need to live the right way during the course of their lives. Some are born into religion. Others have to find it. Most of the message is the same. It is up to a person throughout his life to discern the messages, to solidify his beliefs and to live his life the right way according to what he has learned. God gives everyone that opportunity and judges accordingly. Those that have simple faith will have simple judgment. Those who get caught up in the complexities of established religions may have a little tougher job living up to the expectations of goodness that they have set for themselves. One chooses in his life his level of education, his level of belief, his understanding of the Commandments and what God expects of him. Everyone has a path to follow to save his soul. Although there are trials along the way it is up to each individual along this path whether or not he accepts Evil as a part of his life.

In your society today Evil has become very strong. It

ebbs and flows at different times. It has been stronger and at times completely taken over some societies. But Evil is not the ultimate power. God is the ultimate power. Since the beginning of time, in order to be with God, God allows souls to choose to be with him. You must understand that for some of you, earth is a test. Your life is the test of whether or not you choose to be with God. Take this very seriously. God is merciful in the view that good people will not be destroyed by the Evil around them. Ask for God's help and it will come to you. But you must be careful, because in this life you are subject to the constraints of time. You need to allow yourself the time to prove your intentions. This is why I have used the metaphor that your soul is being drained. When you stand before God with an empty cup, how can He believe it was your intention to lead a good life. How can God tell that it wasn't fear that made you say, yes, I'll be good, please God, save me? If you spent your lifetime cheating and deceiving people, what makes you think that God will accept you into heaven? God is merciful. He is not stupid. If you have nothing in your soul, if you are drained because you have accepted evil, you can expect no mercy at the time of judgment. When Jesus came to earth and died for your sins, He died for your sins, not for your bad choices. I bring you this message in the spirit of God's mercy to give you a chance to reject Evil, to renew your intentions, to work at filling your souls and to fight Evil. God will not let Evil overcome the world. It won't happen. He is a merciful God. He is a just God. But people must realize that justice and fairness are not the same.

CORPORATIONS AND BUSINESS

Work needs to be meaningful. It must have direction and be properly compensated. For example, The Teacher says that working at a restaurant is good, but that being a telephone solicitor for magazines is not. Earning $5 million a year because one makes the best widget on the planet is good. Earning $5 million because one plays basketball is not. Some will say this is our free market economy at work. The Teacher says it's corrupted. The problem, she tells us, is that our values are out of balance. They have gotten out of balance because of evil. Evil has corrupted our system.

Basketball is a bunch of men running back and forth across a room trying to get a ball through a hoop. It is a game. It is certainly not more important than teaching our young people the skills they need to survive. Yet the money involved with this game and the attention given to players distract such a large number of our youth that it approaches a supernatural plane. It is absurd that we reward the skill of running back and forth with a ball with such enormous sums. We are holding this up as an example for our children. This is wrong. No wonder they are confused, distrustful and amoral. Sport is not work. What we have made sport into is wrong. The people doing it are wrong. The owners are wrong. The fans are wrong. Sport is a distraction. The Teacher says that it is fine for people to be professional athletes and do their best, but they can do just as well earning $80,000 a year. The huge sums of money involved are corrupting an otherwise healthy activity. This creates unrealistic expectations in our young. It ruins their sense of balance. Running back and forth bouncing a ball is a good skill, but any seven year old will tell you that it is not work.

True work is using the talents that God has given. Work should help the society advance because each member is doing his part and using his talents. Work gives us meaning. It is a part of people's growth. It is necessary for development and satisfaction.

Work needs to be more than pushing papers. Work must accomplish a goal. No matter what your work is, the end result should be that it helps somebody or the society overall to advance. Many today feel they work very hard. Yet at the end of the day they cannot see what they have accomplished. Work should provide satisfaction to those who toil. If it does not, then it is not being done correctly. Work should give a good feeling. If it does not, a person should not be doing it.

The force of evil is always looking for an opportunity for control over a person's will. Today's environment is often a breeding ground for evil. Often people do not really know what they do in their jobs. They feel controlled and manipulated. They turn their lives over to a soulless corporation and do its bidding in the pursuit of ever-expanding profits. Greed is the god of the corporate culture. The Teacher says this is wrong and needs to be changed.

People do not need to do physical work to accomplish good. Because of the complexity of our society it is often necessary to have many layers of support people. But everyone should have a goal or task to accomplish.

Here are some examples. Most advertising is wrong. A major soft drink company will spend millions and millions of dollars for personal endorsements, for TV time, and for people to create a visual image that lasts only a few seconds. The goal of this expenditure of time and effort is to produce loyalty among consumers. Yet, if the product is good it will stand on its own. All the effort is wasted of those involved in the work of creating this advertising. At the end of the day they have helped no one. Yet, they have spent huge sums of money to sell a product that people would buy anyway. Advertising in itself is not bad, but the mentality in our society that we constantly need to outdo someone else has escalated the art of advertising to ridiculous heights. People involved in these efforts are not doing real work. They are being manipulated. They are being drained and they are being used as the tools of evil. We need to remember as we are bombarded daily with advertising to see past the manipulation in order to judge a product on its merits alone.

Capitalism is good. Giving people a reason to live and a way to take care of their families and to grow in strength by using the talents God gave them is good. Yet the people who own companies that produce products need to be aware that they have a responsibility to care for their workers. They must walk a fine line between control and supervision. Employees need to be supervised. This is the work of employers. It is their job to make sure that the workers know what they are doing and why they are doing it, and how the work they do and the product they make helps society. But many people lose sight of this and want to use their power to control the lives of their employees. This must be guarded against.

Many times the situation grows slowly. With success come the temptations of money, position, power and influence. Gradually, employers begin to want to control the lives of workers. They begin taking more and more time away from them and their families. They put excessive constraints on them and attempt to make them dependent. Eventually, they may begin asking workers to perform tasks that are unethical and perhaps even just plain wrong.

Perhaps you have worked for such a person. It is doubtful that you were aware it was the force of evil that was draining the boss or the supervisor or the head of the company. Now you will be in a position to recognize the signs. Little by little the will of the individual is replaced with a vision of power or greed. You will notice that their lives are empty. You will notice that they never have enough; are never satisfied. No matter what you do or how hard you work, it is never good enough for them. Although these people continue to function in the company, their efforts no longer are actually work. They have been taken over by the force of evil.

Each of us continually needs to check our motives. Certainly, some tasks are so long term that they might take a lifetime. Nevertheless, every single day each of us needs to examine our conscience and to answer the question, "Are the talents God gave me being used in the best way? Did I help someone today? Do I feel good about what I am doing?"

God takes care of all of the animals and living things. He gave humans souls so that each of us would have the presence of God within. Corporations, on the other hand, have no soul.

Humans are lesser spirits than God. By forming groups, through churches and other associations, humans become a stronger force. The force generated has more energy than the sum of its parts. On the other hand, anything that man builds or creates is inert. It does not have a soul and cannot live on its own. It cannot do anything without the energy that man puts into it.

People try to become God by creating corporations. The

Teacher tells us this is against the natural order and that it is doubly against the natural order when a system of government recognizes this man-made entity and gives it rights. People wonder why corporations do not work, why businesses that are corporations are so hard to manage. This is because they go against the natural order.

The natural order is for man's work to be meaningful. Man should be in charge of his work. There is a common saying in society today that one works for a corporation. The essence of that statement is wrong. Man should not work for corporations. Man should work for man. A non-living, soulless entity is a breeding ground for evil which will suck the life from man and give nothing in return. It demands everything from humans and has no loyalty and no regard for life. This is why it is unnatural and wrong for people to be a part of this system.

The system that is right is the family-owned business. People truly need to be responsible for their actions. They should not attempt to hide behind a corporate veil. If you do something you are proud of, you should put your name on it. The Teacher says it is ridiculous to say that corporation can stand behind its good name. What do most business names stand for? A collection of letters, obscure names, symbols that change when the winds blow. The names have no meaning, no life. This does not mean that an individual or family cannot have a business as big as any corporation that exists. If there are investors that wish to get behind a particular business and support it, that is good if it is the will of those people.

This society has decided to use corporations as a means of doing business. The society will continue and it will slowly prosper but it will not prosper as it could. It will continue to be plagued with nagging and unanswerable questions until it comes to the realization that what it is doing is wrong. This is why there are so many management techniques and books on the subject of managing corporations to the point that it boggles the mind. Many contradict each other. They go in circles by offering the same basic techniques but constantly giving them different names. Not one of them solves the problem because the concept itself is wrong.

The management techniques that many people use run contrary to human nature. It is human nature to want to belong. People want to identify with a group. When the organization becomes so big that people lose the feeling of having a special place within the group their sense of belonging fades. Eventually, the ties are broken. People no longer have an emotional stake. Their only tie becomes money and money is not a good basis for a relationship. This is at the heart of what is wrong. Because a corporation has no soul, it cannot express love or care, or foster a sense of belonging. People do not feel an implicit contract with their employer. The larger the organization becomes the more difficult it is for employees to have a sense of belonging. Yet, the owner of a small business will share a sense of belonging along with his employees. This is how it should be.

From time to time large corporations are broken into small, autonomous groups. This is a move in the right direction. This helps motivate employees by creating a more focused and fulfilling enterprise. The final ingredient needed is the correct frame of mind for the business itself.

In the natural order employees work to make a living for their families by making products or providing services that improve the lives of others. These employees enjoy satisfaction because what they do has value. This is the right attitude for a business. It is what God intended.

An employer's job is to apply the talents of employees in a way that multiplies their value. The worth of the group should be greater that the sum of its parts. It is an employer's job to focus his workers on a goal, a goal they can see and feel and achieve on at least a yearly basis such as a harvest. It is the employer's job to be able to bring the people together along with their families to let all know what they are working for.

The most basic understanding is that workers work for each other and that they work together to make the lives of all they touch better and more fulfilling. When the harvest is collected at the end of the year, God traditionally asked the employer what he had done with his talents. A certain amount was given to God (10%). Then a portion was set aside to buy the goods and materials to do next year's work. The third portion was given back to the community that gave the business life. When this order is realized management is satisfied. This is the highest order.

The natural order is for people to work in relatively small groups. Depending on the business this can be 15 people or 2,000. (In building an ancient pyramid, 2,000 certainly would not be too many. For a hamburger store, 2,000 would be excessive.) People in a group must understand who they are working for and what goal they are working toward. For example, a group of people working in a hamburger store knows and understands the people they work with. They should have time during the day to talk to one another, to learn about each other's dreams and families and to build relationships based on the goal of feeding those who come into their hamburger store each day. Every morning the goal is simple. Feed the people that come into their store. That's it. No greater good or glory exists for them to achieve.

The above group will no doubt be a difficult one to manage and lead. First, if the management of the store is not someone who works in the store, this individual will not understand and know the employees. If this indeed is the case, the employees are working for someone else's good, perhaps the investors who own the store. They will have the gnawing feeling their labor is supporting people outside their group. This will undermine the cohesiveness of the group and its morale. Let's say that on top of this, management places unrealistic goals on these workers by telling them that theirs is to be the best store in the metropolitan area. It is expected to have the biggest gain in market share, to have the fastest order fulfillment rate and to return the most for its investors of any store in its category. The Teacher tells us these are auxiliary goals which should not be made to be important. They are non-essential aspects of the business. Creating recognition for the achievement of them removes a worker from an understanding of the true value of the work he does. The correct idea is for workers to work for their families, not for investors. This is the natural order.

What The Teacher is telling us makes a great deal of sense. There is a growing awareness that corporations do not care for employees. This makes the managerial task ever more difficult. If a business wants to succeed, it needs to pay serious attention to its employees. The business must have a soul. It must have someone in charge who is both accountable and responsible. A publically traded corporation cannot meet this requirement because such a corporation exists for one reason alone and that is for its shareholders to make an attractive return on their investment. The workers of a corporation are mere cannon fodder in the scheme.

This situation needs serious thought and thoughtful action. Employers need to be accountable to God. They need to be accountable to the people who work for them and to the community which supports the enterprise. When those three aspects come together and work together the natural order is fulfilled. The business will grow and prosper as a result.

Some are sure to wonder, if this is the natural order and corporations do not follow it, why do they seem so successful? Why do they make so much money?

The answer is that evil is at work. Evil rewards immediately and well. To be sure, the rewards are not long lasting and have no spiritual aspect.

Corporations use people. The people must give over a certain portion of their free will to the corporate entity in order to make it work. When they give over and are no longer in control of their lives, who is it that they give over to? People will say it is the corporation. But who precisely is the corporation? The corporation is no one. Yet, it is an entity which has a form of life of its own. It pays taxes. It has judicial rights. It can sue or be sued.

If a corporate entity is not dedicated to God, it will be taken over by evil.

Let's say you do not believe in evil. Let's say you do not believe in any spiritual aspect of business. We have a physics problem here. Everywhere on earth, every bit of space is taken up by matter and energy. To exist, and you must agree it exists, a corporation has to consist of something. Yet, no physical matter can be found which can be called the corporation. So, the corporation must be some form of energy.

The Teacher says that in a vacuum of good energy, evil energy takes over.

Let's say we have a corporation that is dedicated to God. It is alive. It is spiritual. All the people know where it is going. The people in that corporation are dedicated, committed and have such an overwhelming, almost blind loyalty, that it defies comprehension. This corporation is the envy of everyone.

Corporations such as this are rare and exist only in religious circles, but that does not have to be the case. Anyone can form a corporation dedicated to God. On the other hand, most corporations are entities without a spirit, without a soul. Most are empty man-made entities and evil is in control.

Whether or not you accept the concept of evil is

irrelevant. It is a force that is at work in your life. It is a force you cannot control in your business. It is a force that will drain you in exchange for money. It is this money that will keep you going. Eventually, the point will be reached where people have enough money and begin thinking, "There must be more to life. What meaning is there? Is this all there is?"

There is more. **The meaning of life is to save your soul**. The soul that this corporation has been draining is the life force you have lost. It is the life force you have given over to a soulless entity that has no life force of its own. It must take yours to survive.

In order to keep people working for evil, there is a system set up in the hierarchy of the corporation that supplies money, power and position. These are the tools evil uses to keep people going. A life of glamor and of travel can also be a life of emptiness. These things have no meaning in the larger scheme. People who are taken over by money constantly have to have more and more to satisfy their needs. This need is created because their soul is being drained. In order to reach a certain amount of satisfaction and fulfillment a person must fill their soul with energy. Energy comes from God. Energy comes from other people. If you do not get your energy from God, you must get it from others. This sets up a system of using others, of controlling their lives, of manipulating them so that they give over control to you, so that you can take their energy.

A corporation is an extremely efficient and effective vehicle for evil to use. The people in charge use it to fill their need of taking energy from others. The people down through the levels of management feel drained. Not only do they have to fight the the travails of their work, not only do they have to fight for their existence, fight to take care of their families, but they feel drained by the people over them. They feel helpless and used. This is why it is so difficult to manage people in a corporation. This is why it is so difficult to show leadership. Leadership becomes "user-ship."

On a different conscious plane from where we humans sit, the plane from which The Teacher views us, corporations are seen as lifeless, soulless entities. They are creations of man which support his ego and his need to be a creator. On this plane, corporations are viewed as a means to control people without anyone having to accept direct responsibility. From the very inception they are inviting evil into the workplace. People give over their own identities to something that has no identity, an identity that has to be made up. It is a force that has been created to outlive men. It is a force that has been created not to die but rather to be larger and more powerful than an individual. No one denies that once created this force exists. Yet people do deny evil. Many deny evil because it takes them over. It takes them over and leaves an emptiness, just as love takes people over and fills them with energy. Both forces are real. Here on earth good and evil are exact opposites with equal power.

A corporation gives evil an umbrella under which to work. The legal umbrella of a corporation gives it more power than an individual. It provides evil anonymity from those who would expose it. It gives evil a life that cannot be destroyed the way a mortal's can be. Corporations are protected under the law, yet are not held accountable the same way as individuals. The good that corporations do in terms of creating jobs and work is seldom equal to the control evil gains by taking over people's lives.

People working in the corporation talk about loyalty, allegiance and "ownership." Yet no one can own the corporation. The mere establishment of a false name and a false identity gives away an individual's ownership. There are reasons for doing this. The biggest is fear. People are afraid of losing. They are afraid of making mistakes. They are afraid of taking responsibility for the consequences of their actions. Corporations are established to limit or remove personal responsibility. From a higher plane of consciousness where The Teacher is, corporations are the feeble attempt of humans to be more powerful than they are. It is humans reaching for some godlike quality which first removes them from God, then puts them on the path of accepting evil into their lives.

Anything that has life but does not come from God, has inherent flaws. Trees do not have to be managed. Forests and streams do not have to be managed. Flocks of geese and herds of elk do not need to be managed. These are things God created. They a part of the natural order and will do just fine without man's interference. Corporations on the other hand and businesses in general need to be carefully nurtured and managed because they are outside the natural order.

This is not the same as trade. People always have traded with each other and always will. The individual interaction which takes place between people when they trade is part of the natural order. It is when people provide something that meets others' needs that the spark of the natural order comes alive in business. But when this is taken too far, when people make more of it than is necessary or proper, business expands to have a life of its own. This is when problems begin.

People will ask, how can a business compete if it is not always trying to grow and be bigger? Otherwise, how can it take advantage of economies of scale?

The answer is, do not compete. You will find that evil is your competition and evil cannot be managed. Evil is the greed and the avarice in humans which makes corporations grow into huge, unmanageable entities. When a corporation gets so large that people do not know each other, when it is so big that all of the workers in the corporation cannot interact with one another, evil begins to come in and take over aspects of the lives of individual workers. Evil imposes an artificial set of standards and conduct by which they must abide. In this way the corporation controls their lives. The larger the corporation grows, the more control it will exert over people and the more powerful evil will become.

Let us look at this in terms of the opposite of love. When a person falls in love, they are filled with wonder and enchantment. They feel as though they can go on forever. They can conquer any problem. Life is full of hope and promise.

When a person starts a new business venture they are often filled with the same sense of love. Why? Because the enterprise begins with the concept of meeting the needs of others. It begins with a sense of the giving of oneself to others. This makes the founder feel fulfilled and happy.

As you read this book, if you have management problems, you no longer have that happy feeling. Many aspects of your life are probably out of control. You are looking for answers that will get you back on to the road to growth. You want to get back into the black. You want the price of your stock to rise. You are looking for profits. Worries such as these are signs you have lost control.

Stop and think for a minute. Where did you lose control? Why is it so hard to make that next dollar? To find the answer, let us return to the higher plane of thinking where The Teacher is. First, let us accept that good and evil are equal powers that work much in the same way, except that they are opposites. Just as giving oneself over to love makes a person feel good, giving over to evil makes them feel bad. Love fills a person with energy. Evil drains it from them. Love makes a person feel as though they can conquer the world. Evil makes a person feel as if he has no control.

It follows that if you feel you have lost control, evil must be at work. At some point you must have given over to it. You do not have to have been a bad person. You do not have to have killed anyone or to have robbed a bank. You simply have to have given over control to someone or something.

Why is it that no matter how much energy you pour into your business or your job, it takes everything you can give and gives nothing in return? The answer is simple. Evil has taken over. How can you possibly manage a business when you have given control to the soulless entity you created?

You cannot manage evil. There are no half-way measures. There is nothing you can do, nothing you can try. No compromise is available that will satisfy the power which has taken over. You simply have to face the fact that your life is out of control and the only way to get it back is to take it back.

This will not be easy. Unfortunately, once evil is allowed into a person's life it does not like to give up. You might think of it as an aspect of your life that is equal to the sum of all of your bad habits. It is as difficult to overcome as it is to quit smoking and lose twenty pounds simultaneously. You are going to have to exert incredible will power. But you must or your soul will be lost.

If it is a business that is controlling you, you must either give it up or dedicate it to God. Either way, you must dedicate your life to God, seriously, earnestly, and in complete honesty with yourself. You must pray for help and be willing to make the necessary changes. If you do not dedicate your business to God, you will have to leave it in order to break the control that evil holds over you. Either option may seem drastic in today's world. But, until you take personal responsibility for what you do, until you are able to know and to touch the lives of all the people you take responsibility for, you will not be fulfilled. You will not be able to manage.

A basic principle of life is the fight between good and

evil. This is the reason we are here on earth. Everyone is given free will. Living is a test. We will either choose or not choose God. All our choices, every decision we must make gets down to a selection of either good or evil. This is nowhere more apparent than in business. In every business decision we must consider how we are serving others. If there is any other consideration involved, a red flag should go up. You are headed down the wrong path.

Consider for a moment which businesses have the highest rewards for the least amount of work. Dealing in illicit drugs may come to mind. How do illicit drugs help people? They don't. They drain the life force from them.

It is a fact of life that there is good and evil in the world. The only absolute good was Jesus Christ. Do not feel bad about yourself because you cannot measure up to his standards. Jesus came here for a specific reason, and it was not the same reason you are here. You are here as a test. He was here to give us the new rules. In essence the rules Jesus gave are to do the most you can with the talents God gave you, and treat others as you would have them treat you. These rules were not a substitute for the Commandments, but an addition to them.

Everyone has to make decisions in his business dealings. Right or wrong decisions do not necessarily have to do with how they impact the bottom line. Using money as your measure means you will be an easy target for evil. Rather, think about the people you are dealing with. Think about your employees and think about your customers. Adopt a long term approach to the way you deal with both. If you do this, your business will develop a positive energy. Others will give back to you. Rewards will come in small but meaningful ways. Your life will become happy and fulfilled. It will be meaningful. Meaning will grow in such a way that you will come to understand that every transaction you make, every encounter you have with others fills your soul a little more. Eventually, you will come to the realization the real work you are doing is the carving of a path to heaven.

What happens to all the people who are rich and controlling others lives? People who do not believe in God? People who do not believe in the principles put forth here are not necessarily doomed forever. But Jesus did say that it is easier for a camel to get through the eye of a needle than it is for a rich man to get into heaven.

There are several ways to interpret this. If money becomes one's god, a person will be distracted from their true purpose, which is to save their soul. If a person begins to feel that they deserve the money they have or that they are better than others because of it, they will lack the attitude that is generally inherent in providing value and service to others. It will be difficult for them to make the right choices because they are blinded by their god. But perhaps most important, if one puts money before all else, he has opened himself to the power of evil. He is likely to give over his free will in exchange for more of it.

This generally happens gradually. A person makes wrong decisions, perhaps a series of wrong decisions that hurts others. He says to himself, "Oh well, what can they do to me?" If you do not make a conscious effort to fight evil you are giving in to it. So don't cheat. Don't lie. Don't steal. Just don't do it.

It takes strength to be a good person. Evil rewards those who are weak. You have probably wondered, why do people get promoted when they seem less capable but more aggressive? Why do most criminals get away with their bad activities for so long? Why is it the least ethical person in the office is the one who makes the bonus, always makes his quota, seems to get ahead of everyone else? It is because evil rewards immediately and it rewards well. Evil knows that when it finds a weak person, that person can be used to corrupt and control others. It uses all the power it has available to make sure that person reaches the highest level of control possible.

This does not mean that all people in positions of power and wealth are corrupt and evil. You must make your own value judgments. And yes, The Teacher says we are allowed to judge. But we should only do so in the framework of our own life and how people affect us personally. It is not up to us to judge whether another person will go to heaven or to hell. We need to judge whether or not they are a good person and if we should follow them, work for them, or have them work for us.

Evil has a great deal of power on earth. It uses that power to influence our judgment and to take our souls. When we get to the point in life when we ask what have we been doing, what have we been working for, what have we to show for life, we are in a bit of trouble. Generally, there has been some influence of evil over us that has gotten us to the point of feeling drained and empty, of questioning the value of life. If you are in business, this is a critical time. If you answer that you are not going to make changes, that you are going to build an empire no matter what it takes, no matter what it costs, you will have reached a decision to give over to evil. You will do anything to make yourself a success. You will attain riches. You will control people. You will gain notoriety and fame. But your life will become totally meaningless. If you are working for someone who is like this, get away from them and get a new job. They have given over. Nothing you can do will save them.

On the other hand, perhaps you will realize that your life has not had meaning because you have not been helping others. It may dawn on you, for example, that your idea of success has been to gain market share rather than to make the lives of others better. As a result, you may decide to dedicate yourself to improving the quality of life for your customers. You ask for God's help.

You have made the right choice. God's help indeed will

come. Management of your business will still be a struggle, but it will be manageable. The feelings of being lost and overwhelmed will disappear. You will be able to throw all of your self-help management books away. You will say to yourself that this is so simple, this is so easy. Why didn't I do it this way in the first place? When you understand the struggle of good and evil and how encompassing it is, when you learn the value of letting your conscience be your guide, business takes on a new dimension. You are no longer involved simply in the struggle of a balance sheet, you are at work in the natural order.

PARTING THOUGHTS

This complex society of ours always is demanding attention. It always has to be played with and finessed and fiddled with. The simpler life that people are asking for and want is not to turn back the clock and live in a by-gone era. It has nothing to do with technological advances. The simpler life that people are asking for is a life with fewer rules and more moral judgment. This is the message that the Angel of North America has for us.

What we have ahead is a complex and difficult task but if we begin and work to do something about righting the mess we have created we can be spared the punishment. The problems will not be solved overnight but we must begin. If we do not start now, however, God will do it for us. He has the power to change things tomorrow. All that will be required is a metaphorical nod of the head.

What needs to be done?

We need to find some good leaders. Moral and just leaders. There has to be a moral base for them to stand on. People do exist who do not have extra marital affairs, who do not lie and cheat and deceive people.

One of the things that is wrong with our society is that we choose most of our leaders from the ranks of lawyers.

This is a group that is trained not to see things clearly, not to use common sense, but to connive and to corrupt the language. There must be a fundamental change in the way we choose our leadership if our society is to advance.

Also, the amount and type of laws need to be reduced. The Teacher tells us it is sufficient to say that one should not steal. There do not need to be 200 laws covering stealing valuable things, stealing little things, stealing cars, purses, money or ideas. It is enough to say, "Do not steal." And, if a person steals, it should be up to a judge to decide what the punishment should be. The problem with making up laws to cover every contingency is that people look for ways to cheat. When people look for ways to cheat, the evil force begins to use them. This allows evil to grow in the society. It grows as people give over to the temptation to do what their conscience tells them they should not be doing.

The Teacher tells us that another thing that must be done is to reestablish the family structure. A family should be a mother, a father and children. This should be the basic unit of the society. Any deviation from this is counter productive.

This does not mean that all who are not part of this type of family unit are bad. What is true is that they have a much, much more difficult life, more difficult than it needs to be. In order not to have a difficult life, in order to have the best opportunity to succeed in saving our souls, it is best to have every possible chance. Bringing children into the world outside a family unit is unfair and destructive to the society as a whole. The Teacher tells us this must be stopped.

There will always be accidents. There will always be problems with people understanding. But accidents and ignorance should account only for a small percentage of the population. Small means two to five percent. Our society cannot grow and flourish with this destructive behavior of fostering the birth and raising of children outside traditional family units. God established family units. Jesus reaffirmed them. Muhammad also made family units the basis of his religion. People must find strength within to overcome the view that anything a person or group wants to do is okay. It is not and we will pay the price for not understanding that it is not all right to do whatever one wants whenever one wants to do it. There is no such thing as victimless crime. The victims are often the good people of a society who must tolerate the increased controls in their life that fighting so called victimless crimes produce. Control over one's life takes away free will. Whether it is given away or taken, losing the ability to choose invites evil into a person's life. The evil force drains everyone. We cannot run from this. We cannot hide. First, evil takes over people. It can take over the entire land.

God has power and dominion over evil, but we are here as a test. We are here to choose either God or evil. As long as we are in our current human state, evil will never be taken away. Man has the ability to fight evil and to refute evil in every form and to purge it from our lives. This is an opportunity we are given. Once we reject evil in every form in which it presents itself, man will move to a higher spiritual plane. This will be the end of the earth as we know it. The prophecies of a New Creation will come true. At that time all the good people will be taken into heaven. Those who are waiting will be judged and a new age of light and understanding will begin for all whom God has created and who have passed the test. This is what we as a people need to move toward. But mankind has a way to go before this can happen. Another punishment will slow our progress by hundreds of years at minimum.

If you do not choose God, that force within you that knows no time and is part of the universal consciousness will not be destroyed. This is what religious leaders through the ages have meant by an all-merciful God. God does not destroy a person because that person does not choose him. Rather, the person's soul will spend eternity outside the influence or sphere of God. What is outside of God's influence is what we know as evil. It is necessary for evil to exist in order for you to be able to make choices using the free will God has given you. Without free will one is not human. If you accept being human, you accept free will. God made you. God gave you life in his own image.

The Teacher tells us that God's image is the ability to think. It is the capacity to love. It is the attribute of mercy and the capability of showing kindness. Being in God's image is to know that you are part of the life force of the universe. God created the life force. He created you. He wants all of the life force back. He wants you back. But God will find no joy in getting all of the life force back unless the life force has the ability to want and to choose to come back, and indeed does so.

There has been a struggle since the beginning of time. God realized at the beginning that some of the spirit he had created wanted more than he had given. The spirit we think of as fallen angels did not know that there was no more to be had, that nothing existed outside what God had created. Nevertheless, God set this spirit free. When these fallen angles received the freedom that they wanted they found that it was emptiness. This was how the force began that we now call evil.

People may not recognize evil. At first evil may seem to be something positive, but it always ends up working against a person. Evil is a force that takes. It sucks a person empty.

Encountering evil is not like hitting a wall. It is not like falling and landing flat on the ground. Not at all. Encountering and giving into evil is like walking into cool water on a hot day. There is no force holding you back.

You go into it easily. Evil accepts you willingly and with open arms. And, like cool water on a hot day, evil is pleasant at first. But evil sucks the heat, the energy from your body. If you venture too far out, if you get into this cool water deep enough, it will weaken you to a point that you cannot swim back to shore. The situation you will then find yourself in can be compared to hypothermia. It saps your energy, saps your strength. It slowly makes your soul die, and it does so without you realizing what is happening, just as being in cold water takes away your strength until you can fight no more. Finally, you slip below the surface, and you die.

It is rare for people actually to make a deal with the devil although it does happen. Seldom does one hear about this because shortly after such a deal most people get what they want and they die. The devil gets what he wants, which is the person's soul. The devil takes a soul quickly after making a deal because he does not want to give the person an opportunity to repent. God is merciful. He is always, always willing to give people a chance to come back to him. The devil, however, is unforgiving.

The devil does have power on earth. He works through people. This is not to say that he puts out a "hit" on someone. Rather, he uses the person's own feelings of guilt and depression. Or he may employ outside circumstances that cause a person to put his life in jeopardy. In either case, it is a choice that people make. When they think they have nothing to live for, they often die. The situation is that simple. There are plenty of psychologists and psychiatrists looking for some psychological explanations for this behavior. They will not find it. Evil is what causes people to take their own lives.

On the one hand, the physical world is perfect in the sense that God makes everything work together in absolute harmony. All physical things adhere to natural laws. But people have a spiritual dimension that animals and vegetables and minerals do not. This spiritual dimension is what brings a force beyond nature into the lives of man. Animals cannot be evil. The devil has no power over them. He cannot make a bird evil. He cannot make a river evil. These things are strictly under the control of God's natural laws. Evil has power in the world only through the hearts and souls and minds of human beings. Outside of the effect evil can have on men, evil has no power.

Evil wants men's souls. This is all evil wants. Collecting souls is how evil attempts to create something out of nothingness. If you do not believe this in your deepest being, you have a tendency to dismiss evil. You are strongly cautioned to do so at your own peril.

All these forces are interconnected: right and wrong, good and bad, love and hate. None of these can be touched in the sense that something physical can be touched. They only can be felt. It is a person's soul that feels them.

People must understand that evil can affect them as much as love. Love is a giving force. One feels love for another person. When that person loves them back they can feel the love directed toward them. Evil takes love away. Evil takes all positive energy away. Evil is an emptiness, a bottomless void that will drain an individual of all good feelings. In exchange for the empty feeling that remains, evil pays with money, power and material possessions. It pays and pays until a person is completely drained.

It is a clear sign that evil has taken over when a person wakes up one morning, realizes they have everything they have ever dreamed of, but that they do not feel fulfilled. They go to work and wonder if this is all there is to life. They have made it to the head of their company by stepping on and using others. They are at the pinnacle. Yet they ask, "What do I do next? Where do I go from here?"

Evil has taken over their life.

Good people whose souls are filling up know that their job is never finished. They know what to do next. They know where to go. When people are filled with goodness and love, they have all the money they need. They do not say, "I need more." They give it away and it comes back to them ten times over. That is the difference between good and evil and how you can know it.

It is difficult for humans to have a relationship with God in the sense that they have relationships with each other. Once a person understands that **the meaning of life is to save their soul** they begin to understand the relationship between themselves and God. In general God has a "hands off" attitude toward the world. It is necessary to allow people to use their free will. That is why they are on earth. There is a saying that if you let a bird go and it flies away, it was never yours to begin with. But if it comes back to you, it is yours forever. That is the relationship between man and God on earth. God lets your soul go to see if it will come back. Once you are born there is no pressure, no direction, no intervention by God in your life. God gives a person life and he expects and anticipates it to come back to him. Not all do.

Our relationship with God on earth as humans should be one of respect, of adoration, of wonderment and of love. It is appropriate and necessary to love the one who has given you life. You need to worship God because he is all powerful. God deserves respect for the wonderment of earth, for the balance and harmony of the creations he has filled it with and for giving us this opportunity to have joy during our testing period.

It is good to pray to God, but one should be careful of what they ask for in their prayers. Humans should not expect God to answer requests. Rather, prayer should be a time for thanking God for what they have. All the information anyone needs to save their soul is available to them. People need to exert effort to find this knowledge within themselves and they need to use the talents God gave them. These talents and the free will to make decisions are what God gives each of us every day. Asking for more is selfish.

Being angry because God does not answer prayers for help is foolish and counter-productive. Bad things happen to good people every day. This is not necessarily God's will. One must see these events for what they are and respond appropriately. To overcome adversity in life is to use the talent, will and resources that God gave you. Overcoming adversity glorifies God. Giving God glory in this way is the relationship that one should cultivate with God.

Often people do not understand why bad things happen to them. Christians in particular are the first to blame God for everything. This is wrong. Most of the time when something bad happens, it is the result of evil working against them. It also is often man's own foolishness for not recognizing and paying attention to the signs around him. In America for instance we often refer to natural disasters as "acts of God." This is a term invented by lawyers which does not endear them to God.

Some time ago people in the Midwest were driven from their homes because of great floods. People prayed. People cried. People were anguished over the terrible things that were happening to them. This was not God's fault. Every so often rivers flood. This is part of the natural order. It is supposed to happen. It is one of the mechanisms God set up for the earth to replenish itself, to renew itself so that no matter what man did, the earth would always be here for man to use and enjoy. If certain individuals decide they want to live next to a river, they must be ready for the consequences. When the river floods, they should expect to lose their homes. If they want to survive they need to get away from where the river is flooding. Blaming God for what happens when one builds his house on a flood plain is wrong. It is that person's own fault, not God's.

Here is another example. In these days and times people lose their jobs because the world is changing. Often these changes come about because of greed on the part of others and the quest for power and position. This is evil at work.

Perhaps a person in such a situation is wondering what they have done wrong. They've worked at a place 18 years and have always done their best. They have kept up with their job, have learned what to do and have always been productive. Then a new boss comes along and nothing they do is good enough. What was good and fine last week has suddenly become outmoded. A person with years of experience and dedication is labeled as one with outmoded ideas. He is regarded simply as dead wood.

The individual in this situation has not done anything wrong and should not blame God for his predicament. This person has come under the influence of someone who has evil working on him. It could be, for example, that the new boss is willing to mistreat people for the sake of getting an efficiency award. That a plaque can suddenly become worth more than a lifetime of achievement is evidence that evil is working on that person.

Does evil have this power? It surely does. The power to work on people to make them mean to each other and do hurtful things is the very essence of evil. Evil is not in the raging river. It is not in the animals or the trees or the sky. Evil can only function in the hearts of man. There can be no justification for any man to ruin the lives of others to win a certificate. The very idea is so ludicrous we are told by The Teacher that in the realm of heaven it is beyond the imagination of anyone. There is no glory in it. There is no honor. Such an efficiency award is so empty an achievement that with little doubt it is the very essence of evil.

Evil rewards immediately and evil rewards well. God's reward comes only after a lifetime of struggle. God's reward comes only after a lifetime of feeling God's energy and love filling your soul. Those who have this energy do not need to ask what it feels like or how to get it.

If you are reading this book and your soul is full and you have that relationship, you will feel a lump in your throat and tears in your eyes. You will be unable to wait until tomorrow to go out and tell someone that you know what God's love is. You will want to share it with them. Sharing God's love is the relationship that you can have with God on earth.

So you wonder, if I have to struggle with evil every day, what is happiness?

Happiness will come to you in a thousand ways. It will come from the thanks of the people whom you help. It will come in the form of sunshine. It will come from knowing that what you are doing is good and from feeling the energy of God flow into you.

It is difficult to know the feeling of fulfillment without knowing the feeling of emptiness. No doubt you have heard stories of people being all the way at the bottom and fighting their way back up from the despair and depression brought on by alcoholism or drug addiction. They have returned from the brink to find love and meaning in their life. You should find strength in these stories and realize the fulfillment in your life in that you have never been in such a situation. It is good that these people have struggled back. But it was not necessary for them to have reached such depths.

Once you have fulfillment in your life, happiness will come. Happiness is knowing that you are using the talents God gave you in a good and productive way. Happiness is knowing that you have sought out and found good relationships with others and that others love you. There is happiness in having children and in teaching them about God, the meaning of life and that they need to carry on God's work. There is fulfillment in knowing that you are doing your part in advancing the human race, however small and insignificant that part may seem to you now. In the big scheme, everyone plays an equal part in God's design.

You need only to look for beauty in the world to bring meaning into your life. It does not have to be the most beautiful rose. You do not have to spend all your time in a museum looking at great art. Take the time instead to look at the precision and beauty of a bricklayer's work. Notice the craftsmanship of a bench or a chair. Regard the structures that man has built using his talents. These talents make life better for everyone.

People today believe they long for a simpler life. What will cure their longing is a life with goals, a life with customs, a life of meaningful vows and commitment. This is what is needed to bring happiness back to our society. These are the teachings of the Angel of North America and the message she brings in the name of God to help each of us have a better life and to save our souls and our society.

AN AFTERWORD BY THE ANGEL

Some weeks after Stephen Hawley Martin began to help us organize and edit this book, The Angel of North America communicated a message to us which I took down verbatim on my computer. After discussion and reflection, we agreed that it puts the book in perspective from the Angel's point of view and would make an appropriate afterword to what has been written. This message has been reproduced here in full with only minor editing for clarity.

The word "prophecy" has two meanings. It means to speak or utter by divine inspiration. It also means, "prediction." The message of the book that you are working on is indeed a prophecy, but not in the sense that what it says [about a punishment] will necessarily come to pass. People have confused the two meanings of the word many, many times.

The purpose of this message or prophecy is to alter or to nudge. It is to make sure prophecy works into the natural order of your world. You see, prophecies can work for two or three or five thousand years of your time, but that is only because you keep track of them. The message that we have to deliver is for your society, now and for the next generation. It is approximately for the next twenty years that this message will be valid, during the time of the people [Pat and Jerry Meyer] who allow us to use them to communicate. It will not last throughout the ages. Its purpose is to adjust the path your society is taking. This path is a culmination of all the individual choices that the people make who form this society. God knows what is happening to each and every one of you. God knows the exact location of every grain of sand. And this is important, because you have free will, because you have choices.

The individual is not important in the consciousness of the society. What is important has to do with the energy that the society has the potential to generate. The extreme importance of this potential is how I can justify my intervention at this time. We do not interfere with individual lives except for those who are chosen [in the biblical sense].

There is a potential of energy that can be generated from the people on earth. That potential is very weak right now. It becomes weak because Evil drains it. Even though everyone is trying to be good, even though everyone tries to lead a good Christian life, the liberal attitude in your society that allows Evil to grow, drains the potential of energy that your society has. This is why we are bringing you this message. God will not allow this energy to go below a certain level. He will not allow free will to be inhibited to the point where people could lose their souls because they do not have the opportunity of choice and free will.

There were societies, recently in Russia, in which people turned away from God. People lived in a society in which they did not have choice. It was a time of great suffering. During this time those people did not prosper. But Evil can work against a society until it eats itself away like a cancer and eventually destroys its host. This is what came to pass.

Because God is just and merciful, his message is coming to your society now in the form of this book. He did the same at the time of Moses. He did not send a punishment to the Egyptians without a fair and ample warning.

This is the message that we have for your society: fight Evil in your time. Fight Evil in your hearts and in the temptations that you face, or it surely will destroy you. We are telling you this because the punishment could happen within this lifetime. There is no time in heaven so we cannot establish a precise date.

Should your people recognize the message, heed the message and make the changes necessary, the punishment will not come. As it was in the time of Moses, had the Pharaoh let the Jews leave Egypt there would have been no punishment. The prophecies of the struggle of the Jewish people would not have been fulfilled. No one would have recognized them and no one would have paid any attention. There would have been no struggle in the desert, there would have been no Passover, there would not have been the struggle of the Jews taking over Canaan. Their life path would have changed how the world is today. Once people understand this concept, they need to heed the message that we bring.

There are prophecies that could and do coincide with this change of the millennium. There are prophecies that will coincide with astrological signs and natural events that will occur. The choices that your society makes now and for the next 20 years will determine what prophecies become valid predictions.

A punishment that God sends to overcome Evil in your society should not be construed as the end of the world. It should not be construed as the second coming of Christ. It is possible, however, that these events will coincide. Heaven help you if they do.

What about those who believe that an Age of Enlightenment is on the horizon? They could be correct if you are able to avoid the punishment. Should your society be successful in changing the balance of Evil in this generation you will be ready to take the step to the Age of Enlightenment. If you are unable to overcome Evil and God intervenes to destroy those who are evil, you will be plunged into a dark age. You will have to fight your way back to where you are now. It may take a long, long time. It may take several hundred years to reach this point again. You see, God will not destroy the earth. He will destroy people. Since God will not interfere with individual lives, the destruction will be very broad based across the society. Those who survive will be those with the best survival skills. In a predominantly evil society, evil people have the best chance of survival, so the punishment will continue until the balance is reached.[1] In a society of hundreds of millions of people, we are talking tens of millions, perhaps even hundreds of millions who will be killed. It is no doubt difficult for the people of your society to grasp this concept because of their liberal idea that every life is precious, that every life has meaning. To understand, they would have to view mankind from a larger perspective where single lives merge into a level of energy. This level of energy is recognized by those of us in spirit. Individual spirits [of humans] will be recognized and judged when they arrive in heaven, not while they are on earth. So the tragedy of losing four million people in a war, six million in a repressive country, or 20 million in a corrupt and evil society such as was the case in the Soviet Union during World War II, is nothing, nothing compared to the punishment that will be sent to overcome Evil in North America.

---

[1] In the vision given to Jerry of the punishment he was shown that some people who are "chosen" will survive because of instructions they receive. God does not interfere in the lives of the vast majority, but he does in the lives of "chosen" people. The "chosen" in Jerry's group of survivors numbered just over 6,000. From this one can judge that the percentage of "chosen" people in the population is infinitesimal. Moreover, when an individual is "chosen" they know it.

There is a prophecy that you will have to deal with an Anti-Christ in your midst. This will represent a great, great evil to face the world. Not just in your society, but the entire world. Should your society not be strong enough, not be prepared to overcome the drain in energy that this demon will cause, you will be lost. What is important to us [in spirit] is that we do not lose souls to Evil. We do not want souls to become so drained that they cannot have a chance for reconciliation. There must be some energy left, there must be some life force in order for God to show mercy. There are people who are so drained, who are so overcome with Evil, that they can take another's life without compassion. They take their own life in utter depression and give up all of their will to drug substances and the inanimate force of Evil that literally sucks the life out of them. People who die in this state are lost.

Should a punishment come, some will kill themselves because they feel that it will be better to be dead than to have to struggle through life. They will be lost. All of those souls will be lost. We do not want this to happen. People have to know what they are facing. This is why I am spending so much time telling you about the Evil. Those who believe that it does not exist are the most apt to fall into its grasp. It is difficult to comprehend the loss of energy.

It is a common saying that when you are dead, you're dead. "When I am dead, I will no longer know. I will just rot and cease to exist." I am here to tell everyone who will listen that is the wrong way of thinking. There is a spirit in each human that recognizes life, that holds on to life, that keeps a person waking up every morning. This spirit marvels at the handiwork of God. No one is so cynical as to not respect a mountain sunset, or the power of the ocean. You have the spirit of God in you. That spirit will not die, but it can be removed. Being removed from the energy is the ultimate punishment. It is a hell that a person creates for himself. A person will still have imagination. A person will still have consciousness. But this consciousness will be filled with a dark and horrible, empty force of evil. The lost soul will become part of that emptiness that attempts to possess and take the life spirit from good people. It will be a part of that emptiness that is reviled and hated and will never see an enlightenment. It will never be with the spirit of God. We do not want this to happen to one, single soul. That is what is important. That is the meaning of life—to save your soul, to fill your soul, and to be with God.

About the Age of Enlightenment, should you overcome this imbalance of evil in your society within the next generation, the liberal view will change and people will recognize what it will take to lead good lives. In the context of time, this will happen very quickly. People will come to realize almost simultaneously how important God is to them in their lives. People will realize how destructive bad behavior is. The Commandments will again become the center of everyone's life. They will not be argued or debated. The Commandments will be the rule and basis of your lives. All of the laws that you have now will pass away because they will be meaningless. People will not lie or cheat or steal. They won't covet each others' goods. Everyone will become successful because you will no longer be wasting your human capital. The Age of Enlightenment will have arrived.

As people begin to shed their laws and not to worry about having to make choices in their lives because temptation will fall away, a utopian society will emerge. The people will become of one mind and turn their attention to where they need to go next. Your concept will be to leave this earth. In order to successfully leave the earth, you will have to get in touch with the energy [of God]. You will find ways to turn your life force into the energy that God has given you. There is a popular colloquialism that describes this very well, "Beam me up, Scotty." This concept is not science fiction. This concept is the end achievement of the Age of Enlightenment. It is the end time of your life on earth. When you have accepted God, when you have accepted God's plan, you will be ready to travel on a journey to the heavens. The prophecies of the Apocalypse, the Anti-christ and a final Judgment will not come true. People will no longer be necessary on the earth.

You can become extinct in two ways. You can die off from an act of God or you make the choice to leave the earth on your own. The second coming of Christ can be Jesus opening the door for you on the other side when you have found a way to enter the energy without dying or judgment. This is possible. But in order to achieve this state you first will have to recognize and then overcome Evil. Later, during this Age of Enlightenment, it will be as simple as making a choice for you to say, "I will not do that. I will not be a part of that action. I will not be lazy. I will not deceive my friend for my personal gain." When these decisions are made, Evil will be defeated. It will no longer have any control over you. People will become filled with the Holy Spirit. The energy potential of the society, and of the human race will be realized and fulfilled. Jesus will come to welcome you because you have made the decision. You have made the decision to overcome Evil and there is nothing left on earth for you to do. The spirit of God will come to you and show you the way to be with him. This will be the second coming of Christ. It is unimaginable now because Evil still has such a hold on you.

For thousands of years you have had to face dealing with control, dealing with laws, dealing with having to be punished in order to be good. You are at the point where that is no longer necessary. Mankind has come to the stage of adulthood. If you are willing to leave your period of learning and to accept the responsibility for your actions, to throw off this liberal view and to take responsibility for following the Commandments, your life will change. It is not difficult to be good, but it is easier to give into temptation. When you realize what is at stake and the potential of energy that is available to you, your life will change. This will be a time of graduation. This is a time of moving forward for your society. It all comes down to taking responsibility for what you do and who you are, or to giving the responsibility over to someone else. God will not interfere with your life, but Evil will. It is up to your society to choose whether or not you will enter this stage of enlightenment.

Just because you are humans and you come to an end does not mean the world will. The prophecies of destruction will be forgotten and meaningless because everyone will be able to make the trip without pain, without dying, to the light that you envision as heaven.

HELP SPREAD THE WORD

Please help save our society by circulating *The Teachings of The Angel of North America.* Give someone this book so they can learn what they need to know to save their soul. Ask them to pass it on when they finish.

Everyone who is willing to listen must be made aware if we are to succeed in correcting the escalating imbalance between good and evil that threatens free will. Please aid our effort to avert a punishment by joining in. You could be the one to tip the balance back toward good, and save our society. At the same time, you can make a critical difference in the lives of your co-workers, friends, family, service club or church members.

To help you and others in this cause, deep discounts are being offered for quantity purchases of this book via our toll free line. Everyone is encouraged to pool their resources so that as many copies as possible will be put into circulation. We have no time to lose.

Discounts are as follows:

1 through 4 copies.....................No discount

5 through 9 copies...........................25 % off

10 through 127 copies......................40 % off

128 (2 full cases) or more..................55 % off

All prices are plus shipping. All major credit cards are accepted. Orders can be placed between 8 a.m. and 11p.m. eastern time, Monday through Friday. Call this number to place your order: 1-800-879-4214.